OBJECTS OF SLEEP

Patrick Hourihan

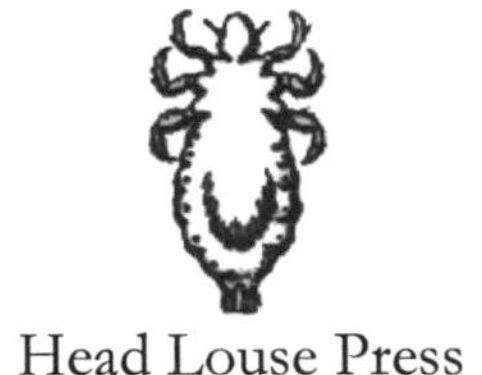

Head Louse Press

Objects of Sleep
by Patrick Hourihan

ISBN 978-1-4717-5218-6

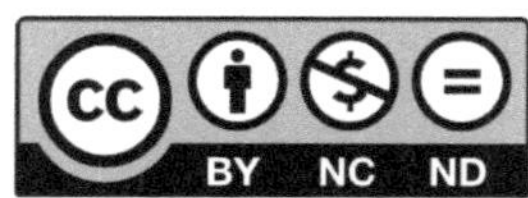

Additional copies of this book can be ordered from Lulu http://www.lulu.com/

To Wayne, for his constant support, love and amazing patience.

To Merl and Paul, my friends and wonderful comrades, always.

To David, a dear friend who is always there for me.

To Fiona, remarkable friend and Queen of Fitzrovia.

OBJECTS OF SLEEP

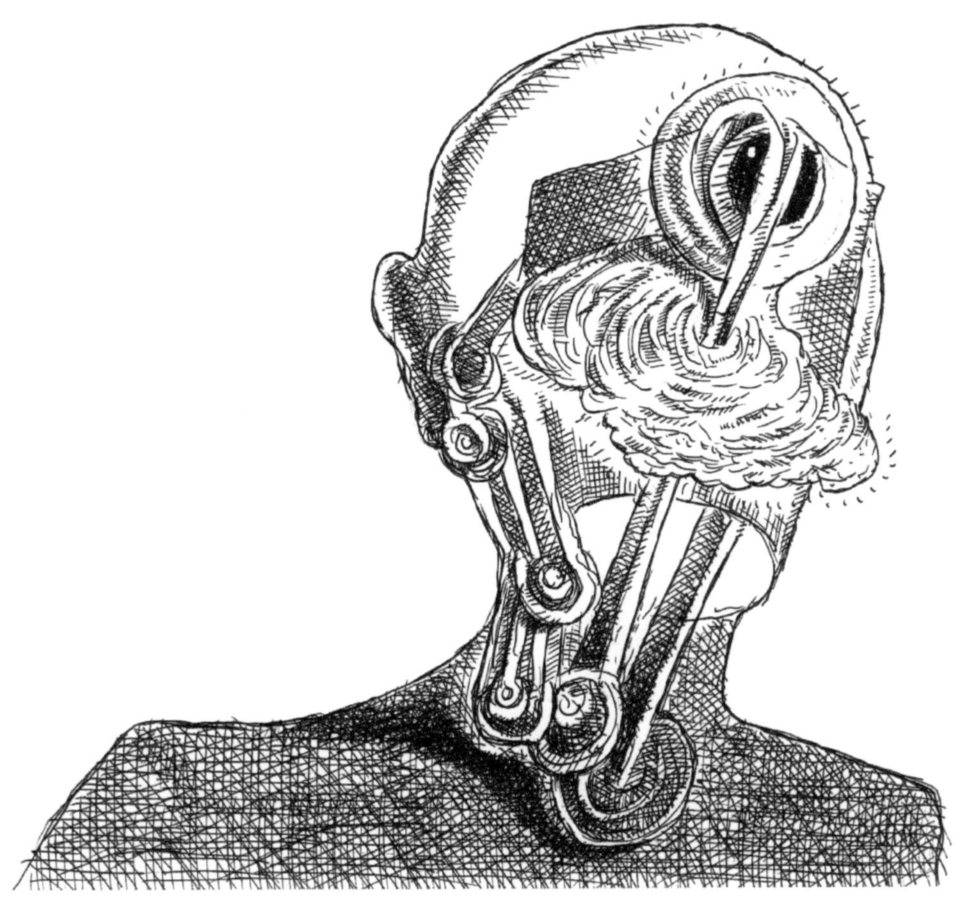

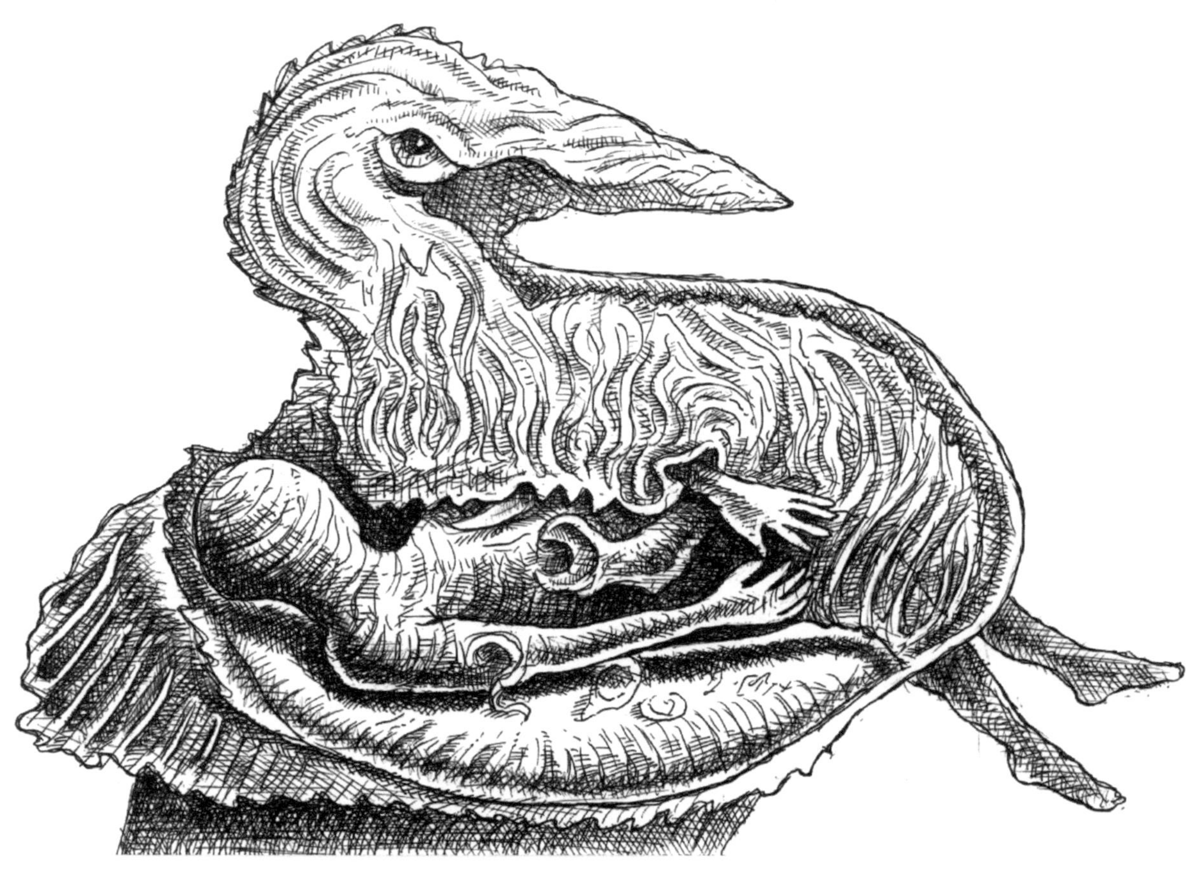

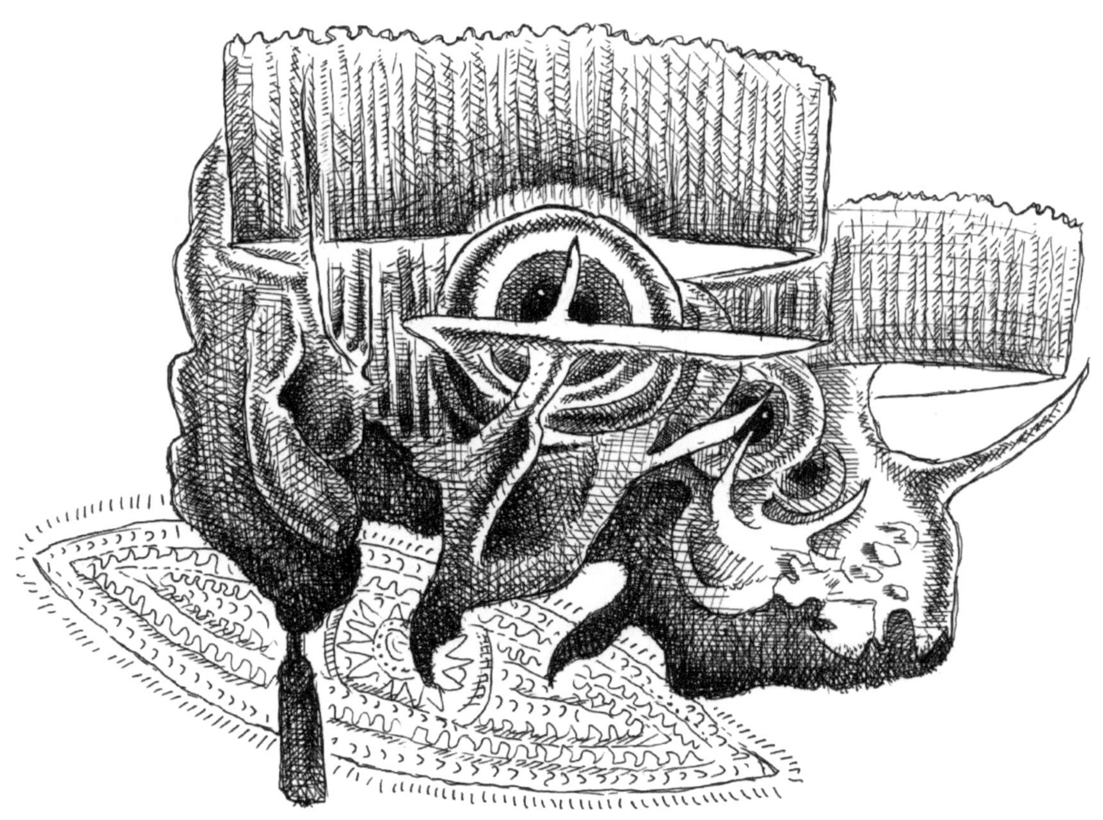

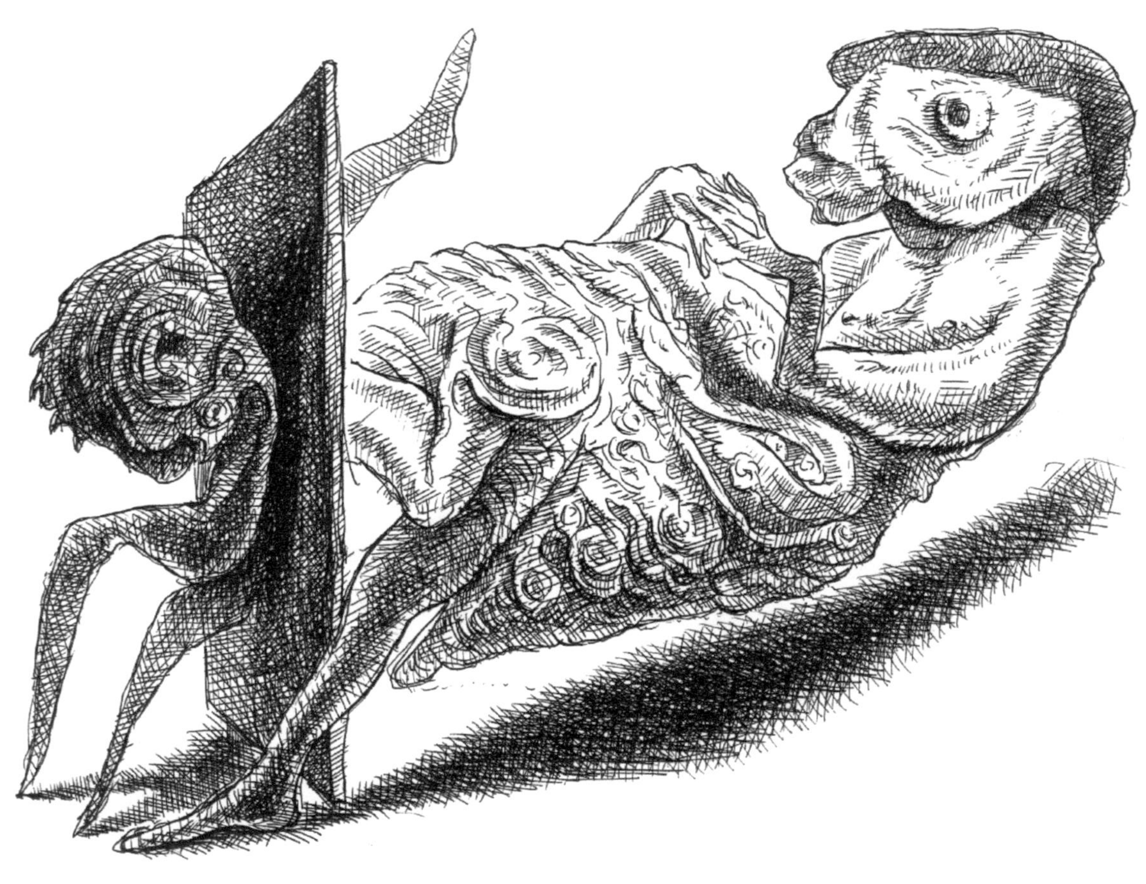

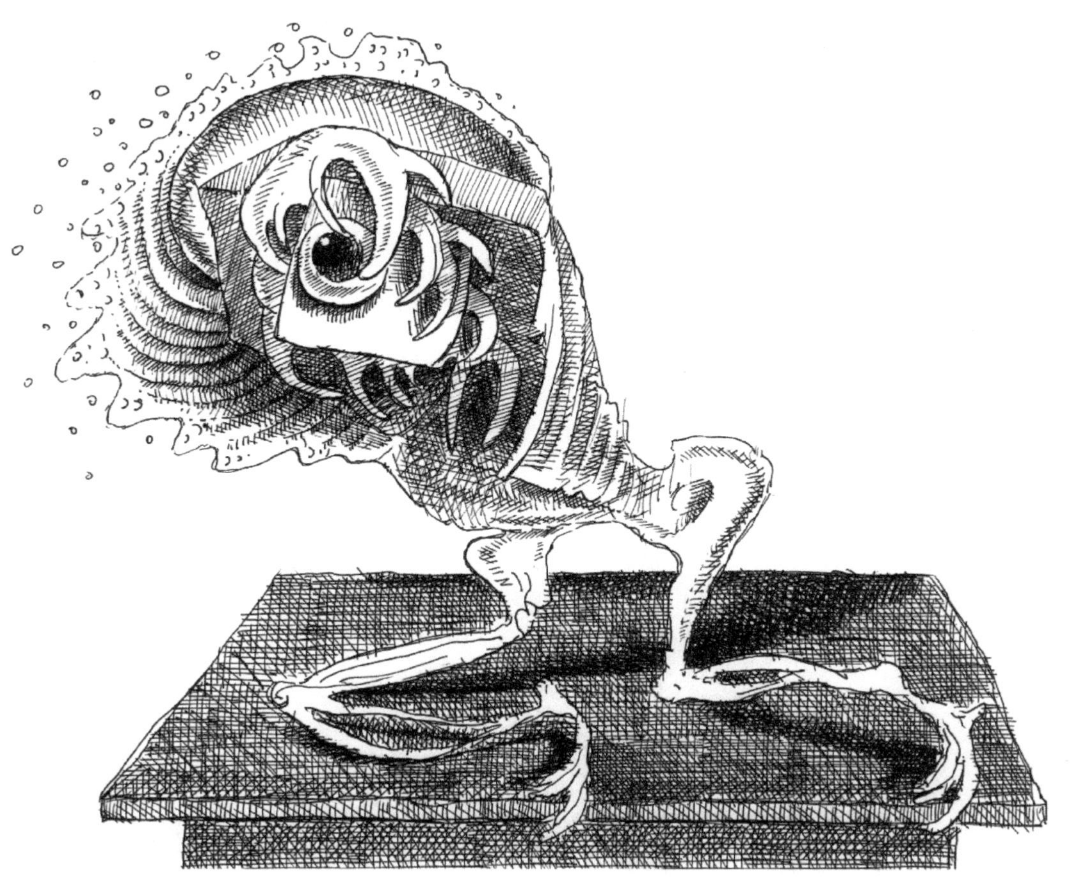

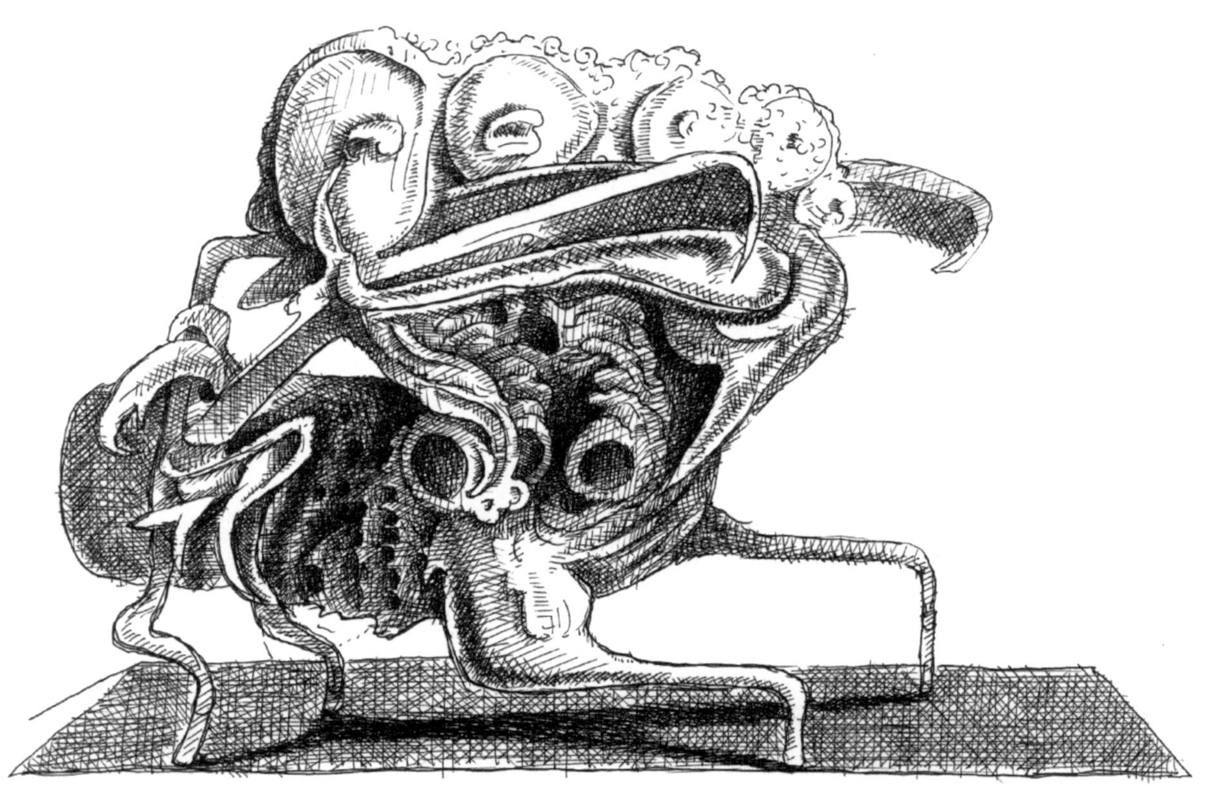

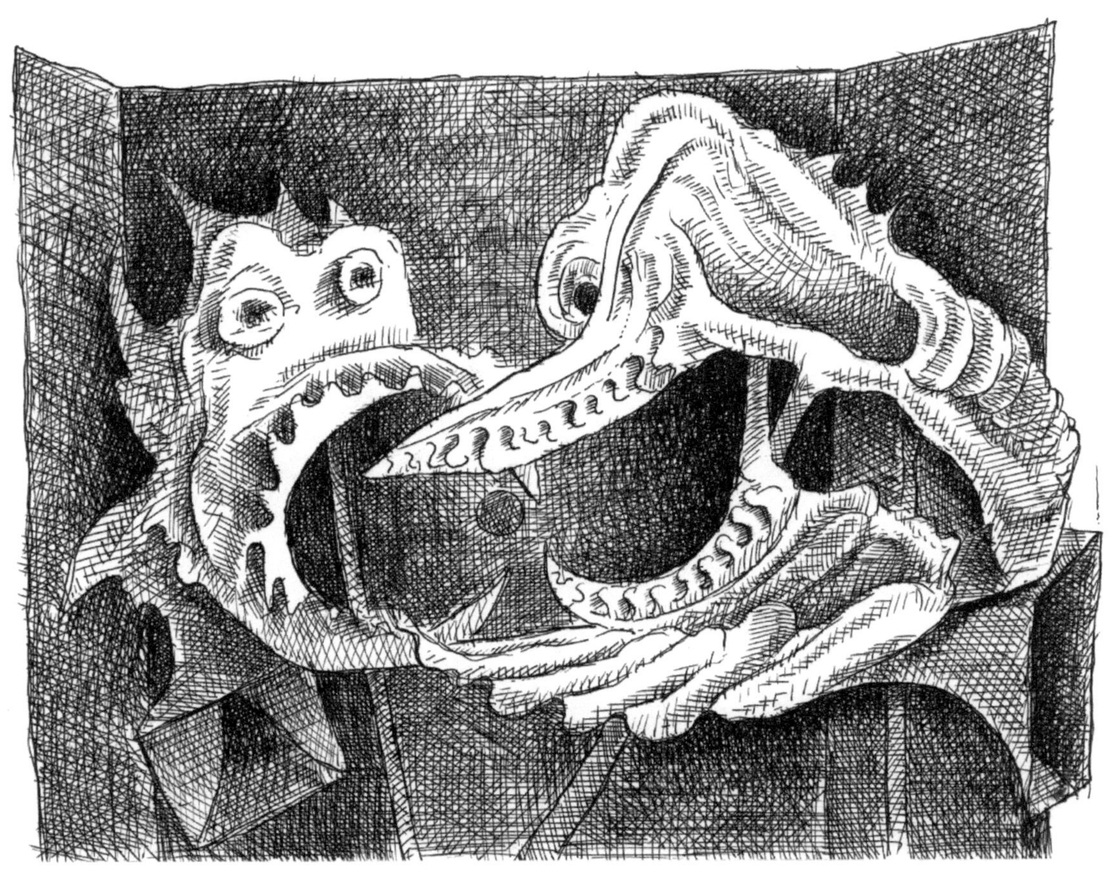

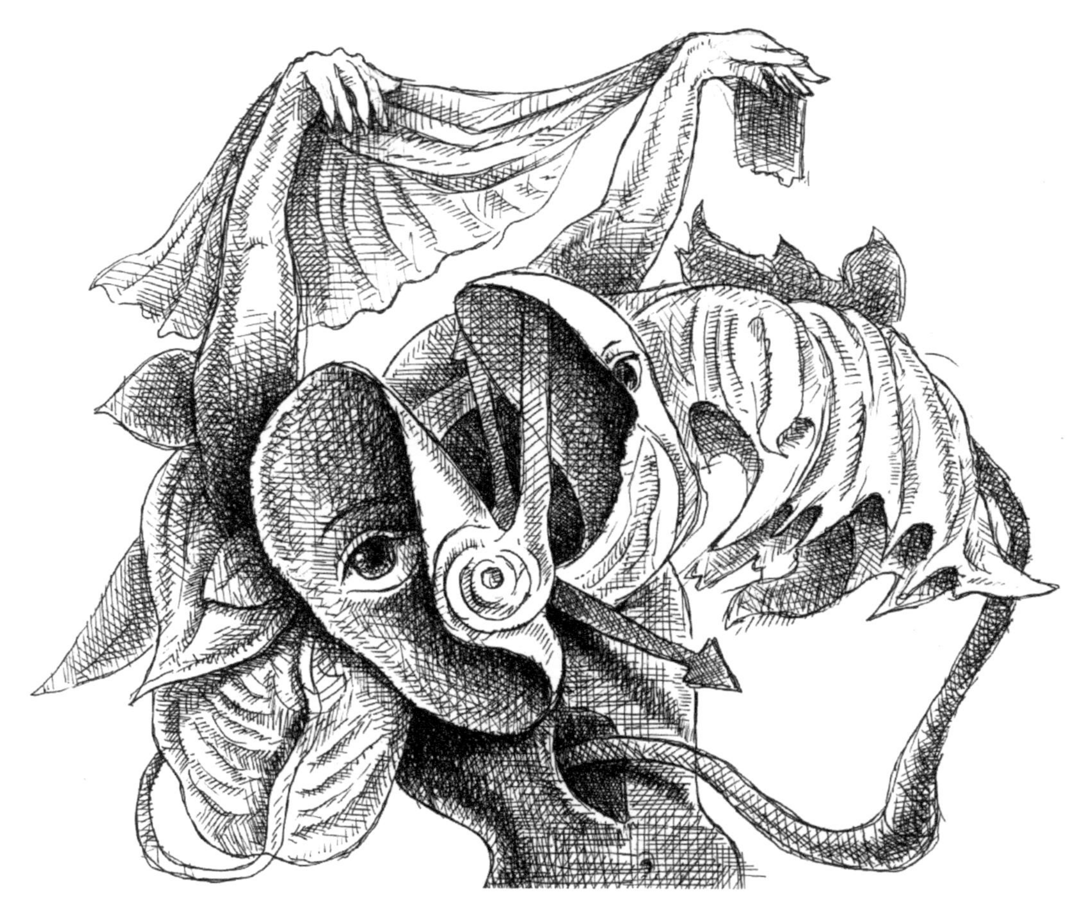

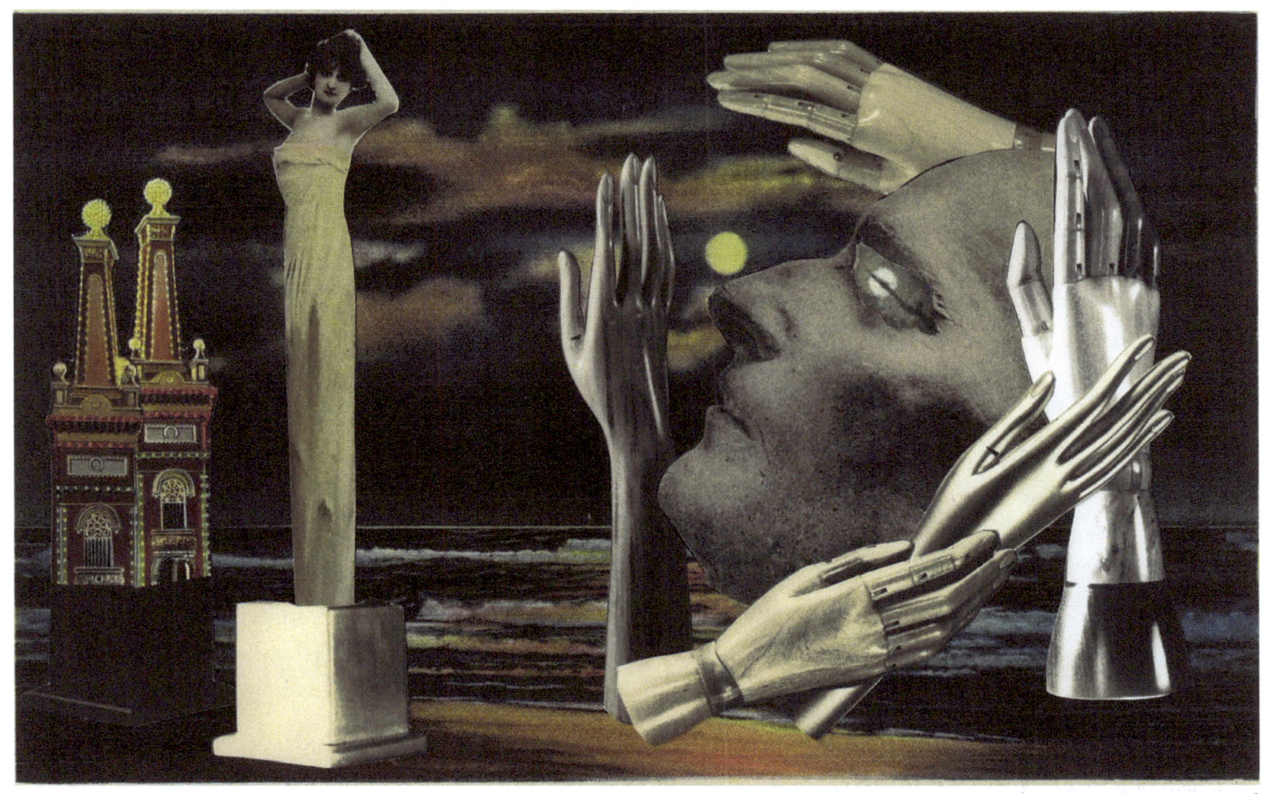

Mermaid

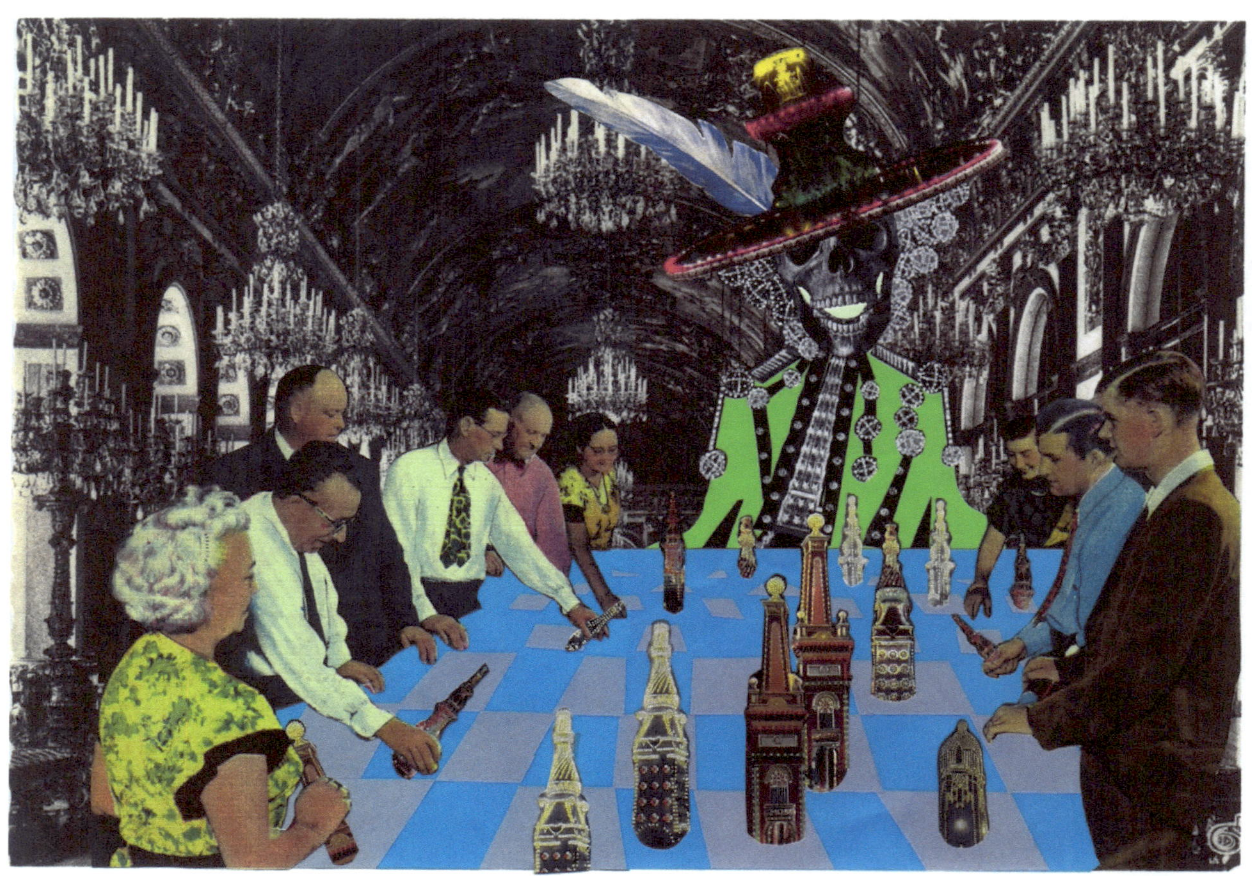

News from the already dead

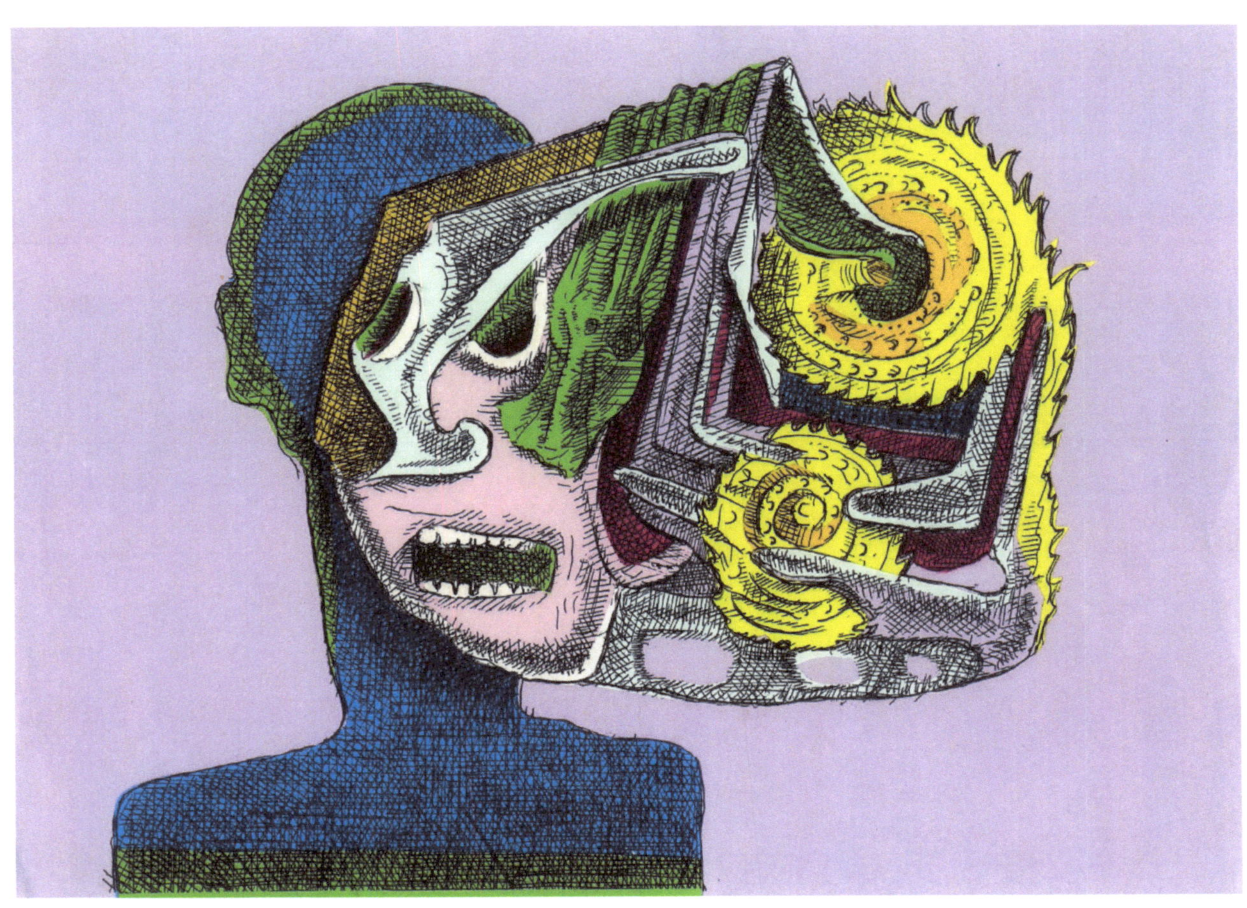

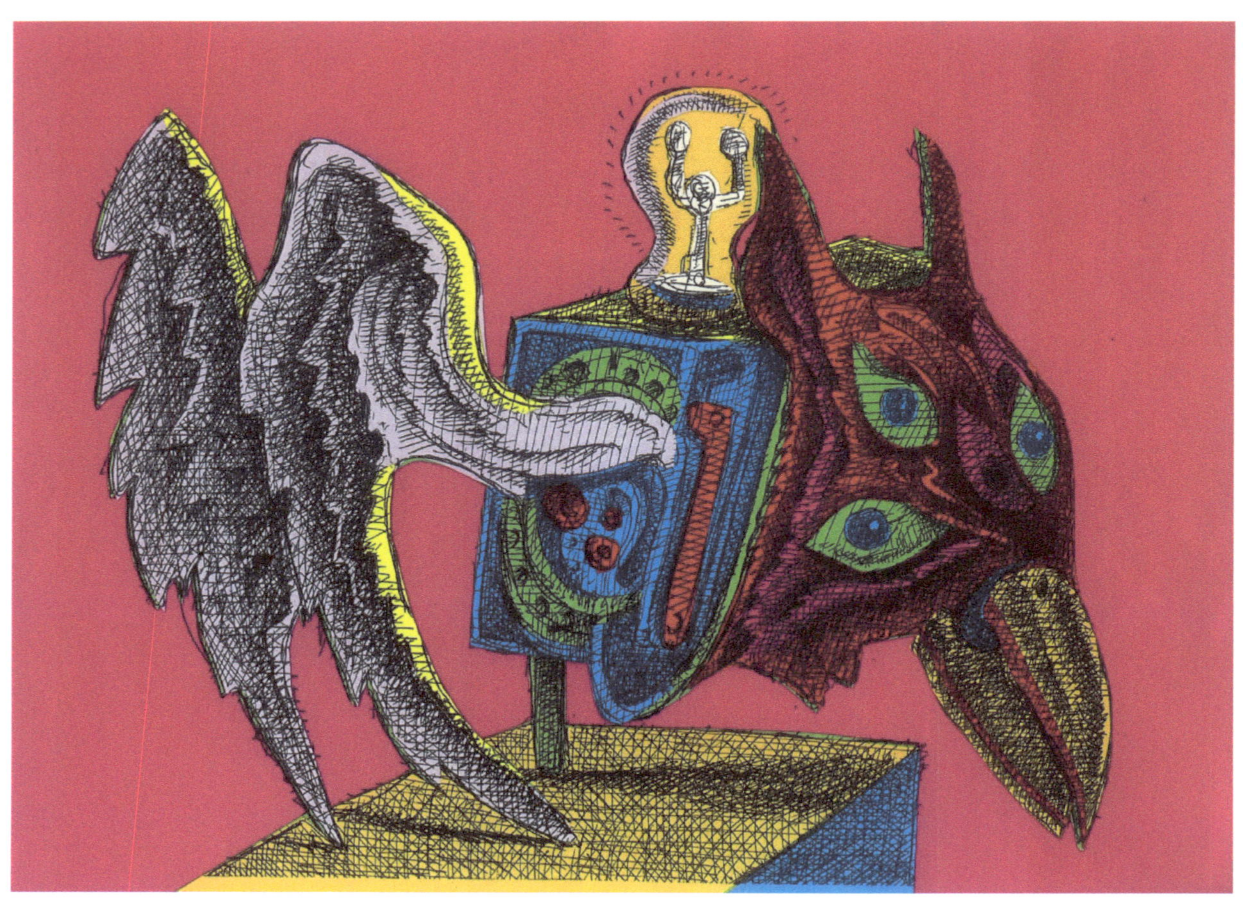

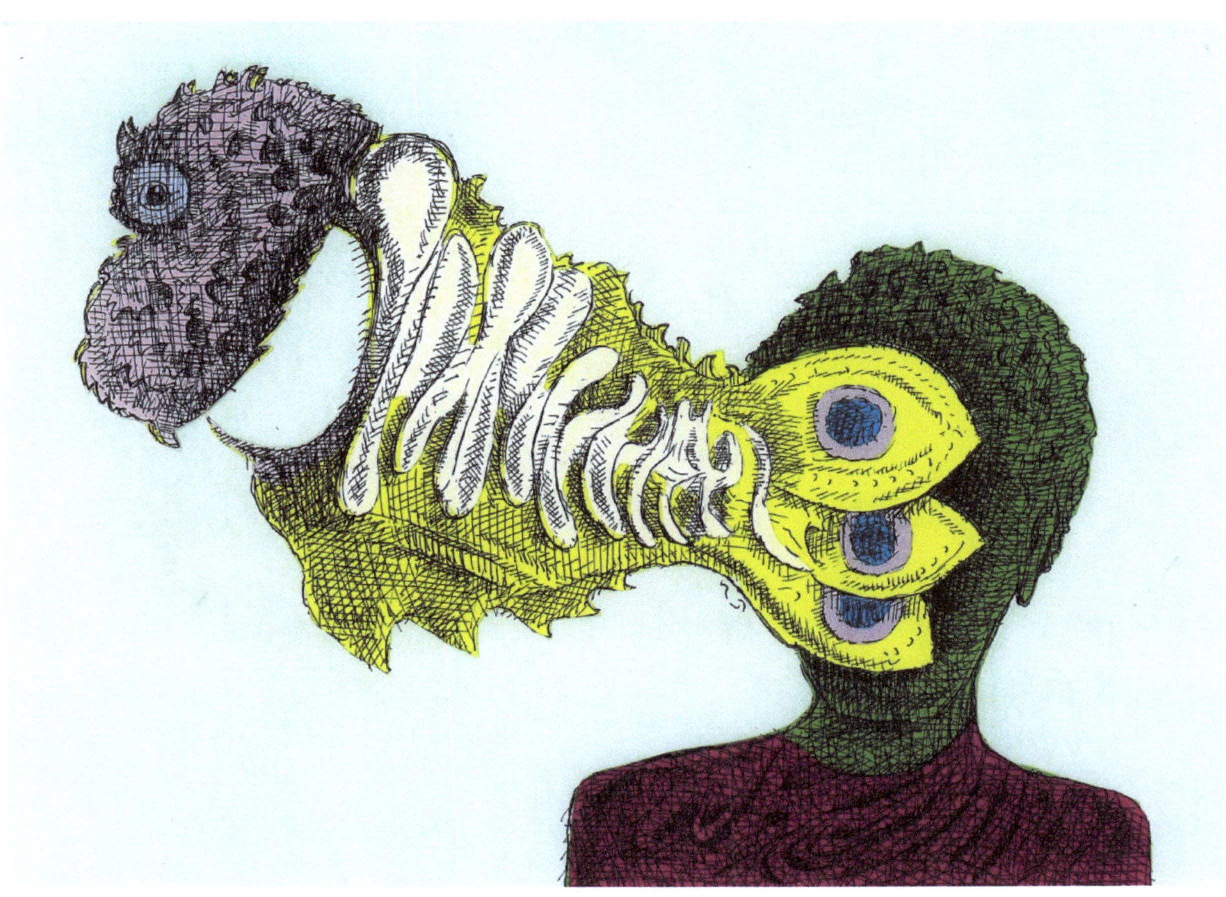

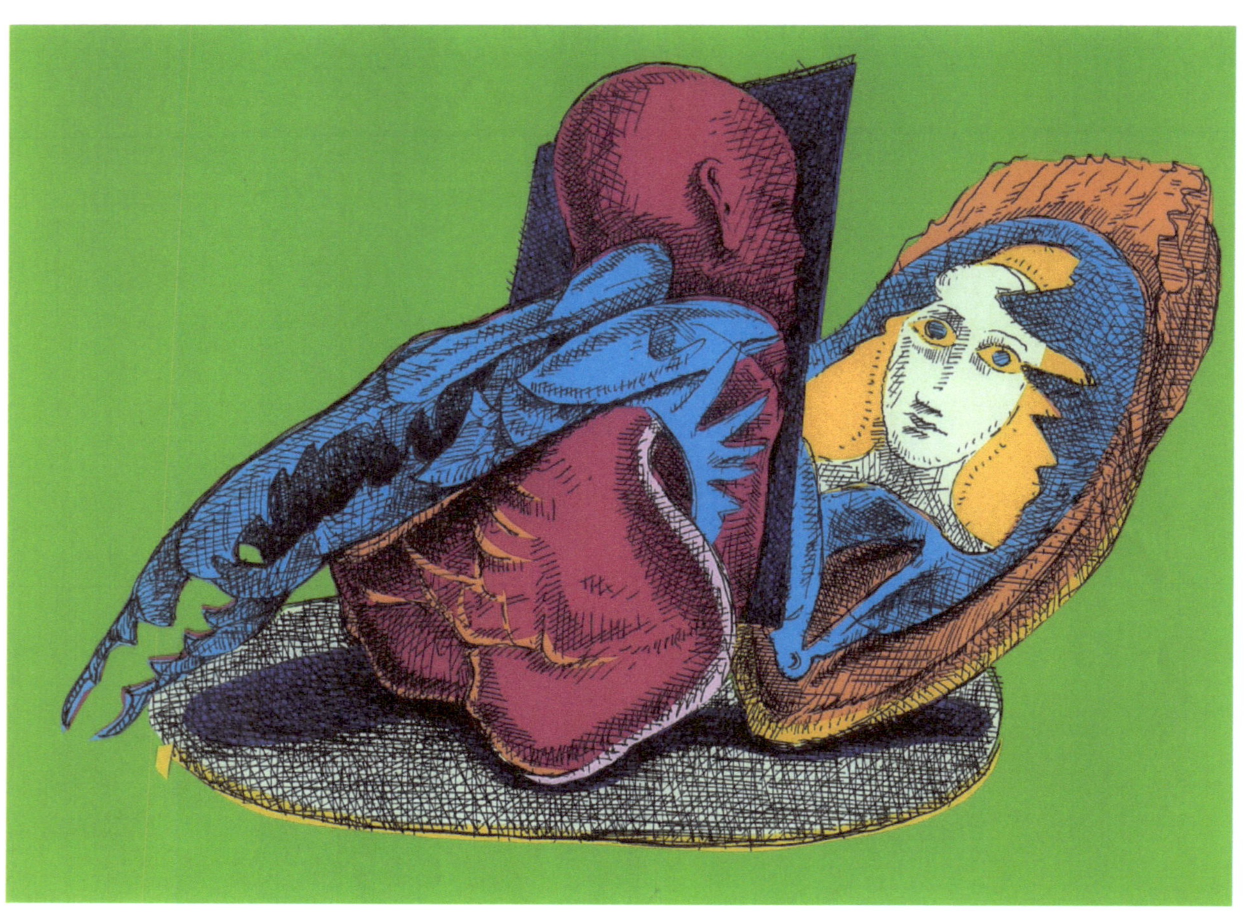

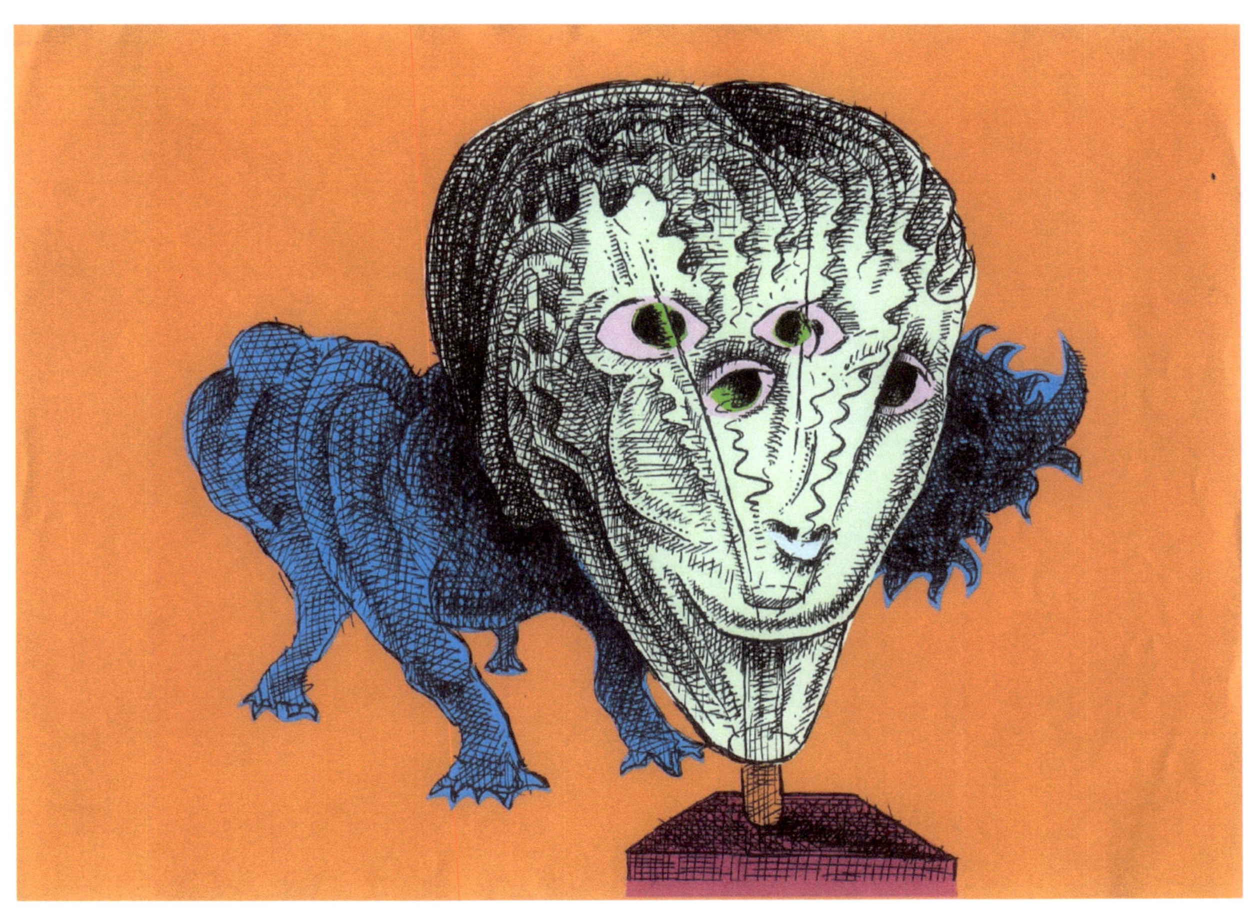

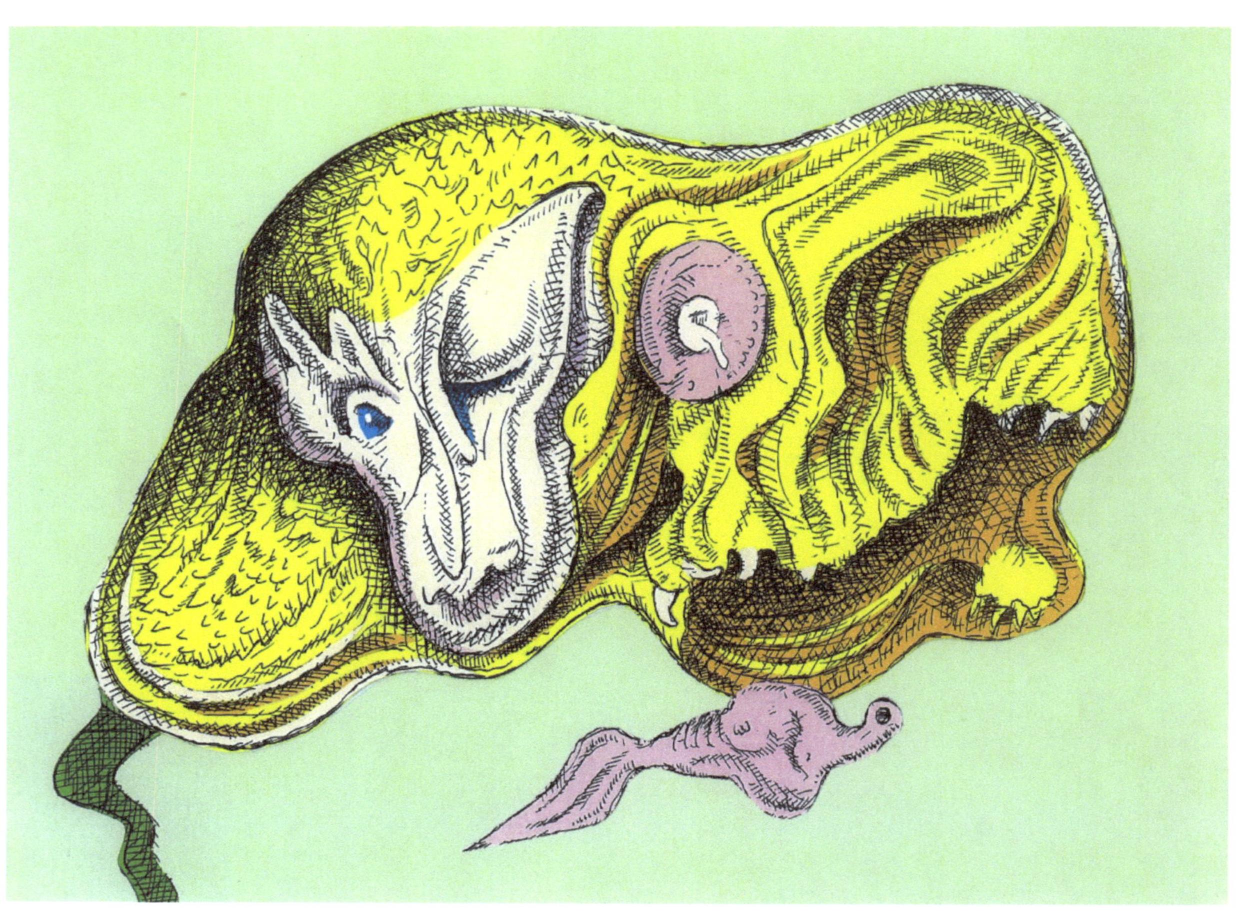

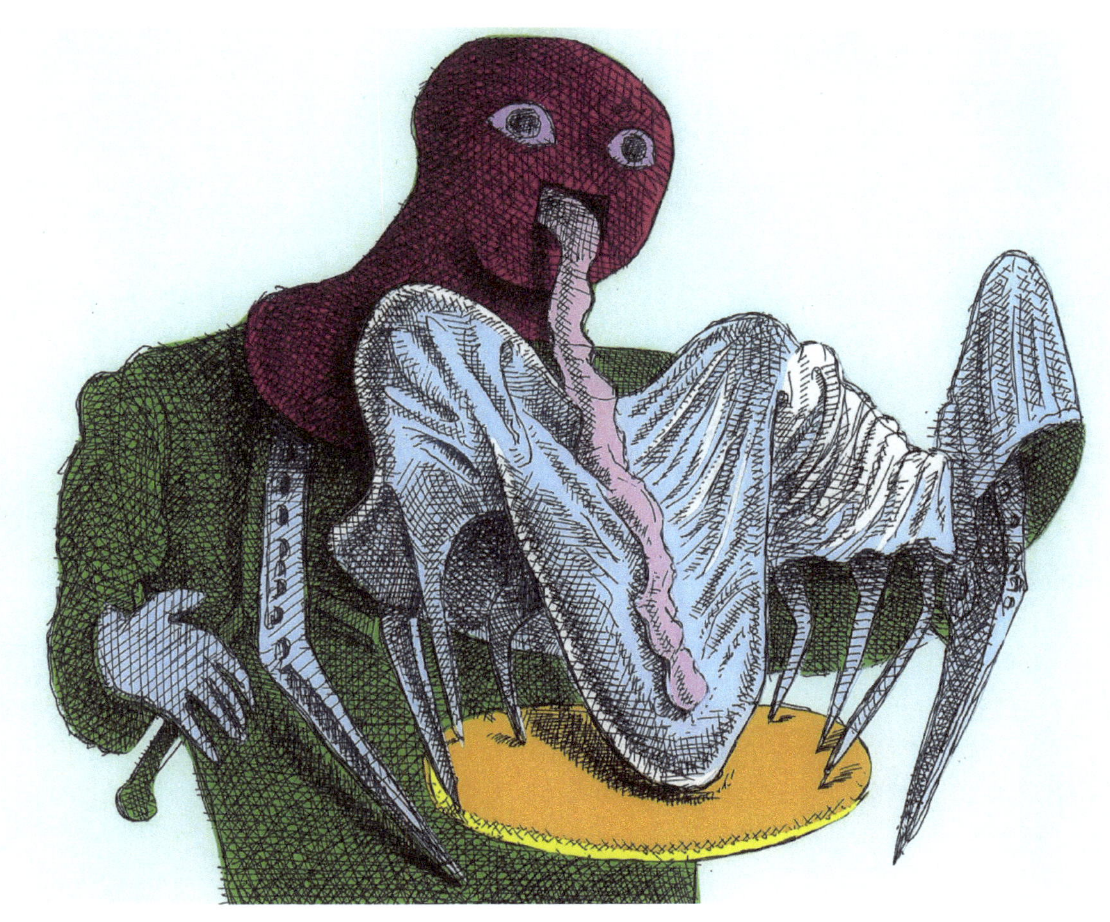

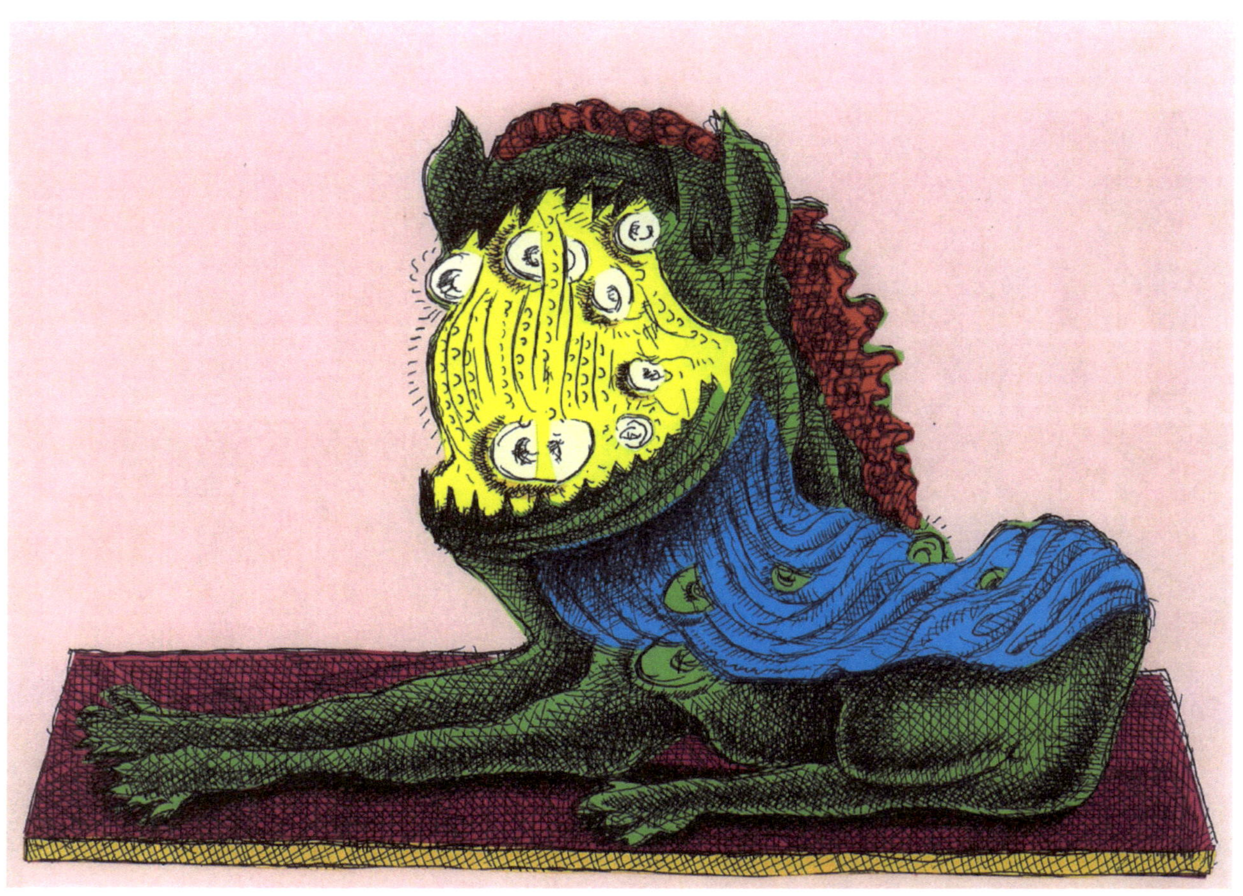

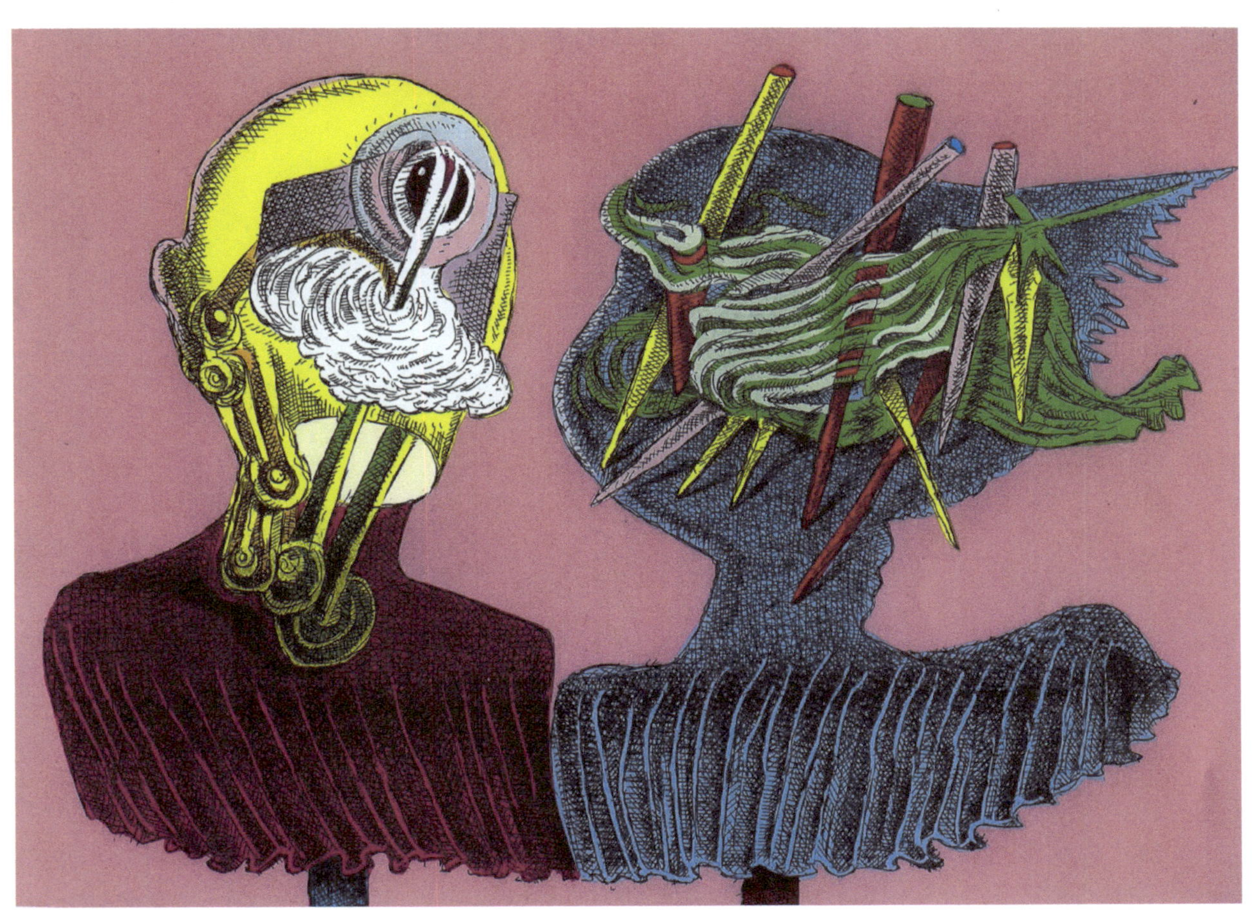

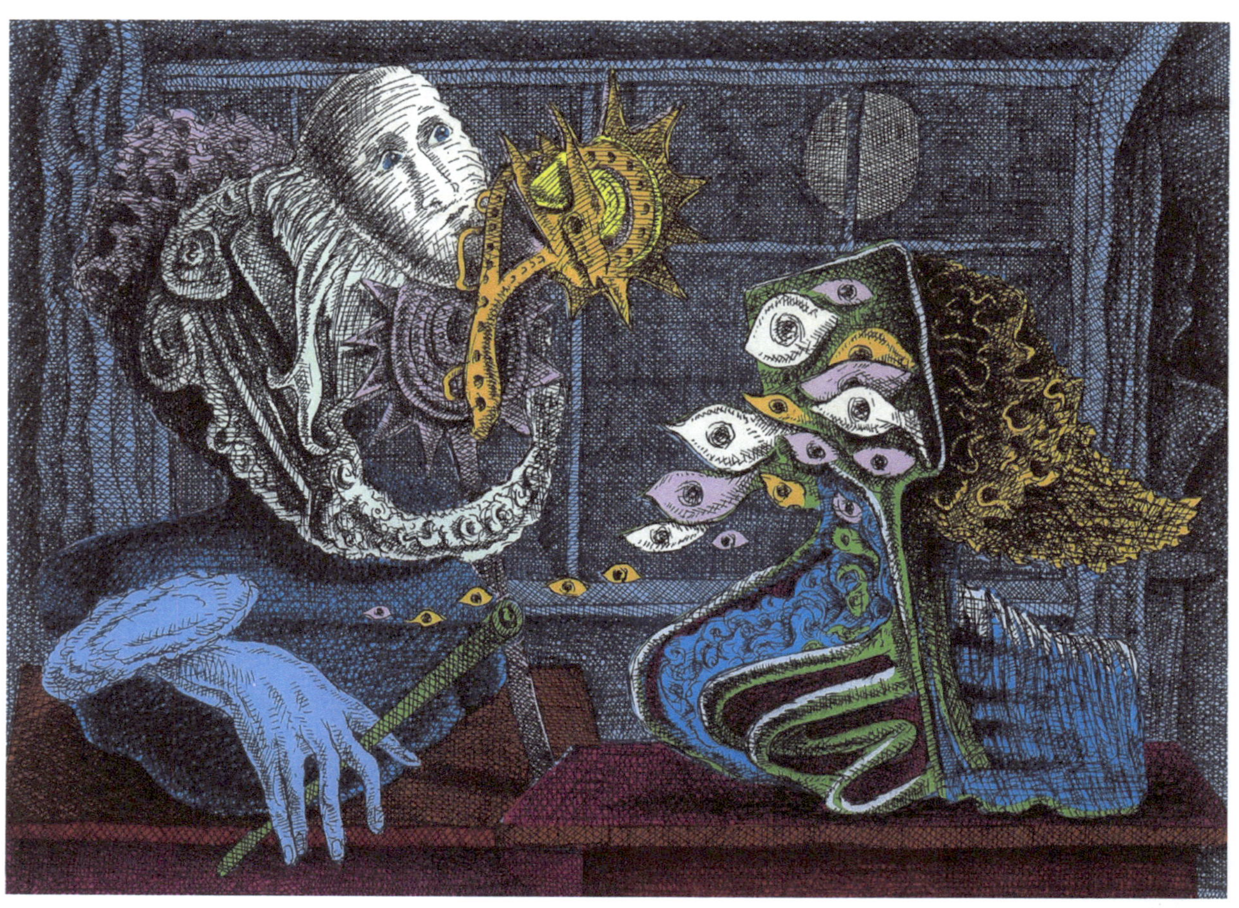

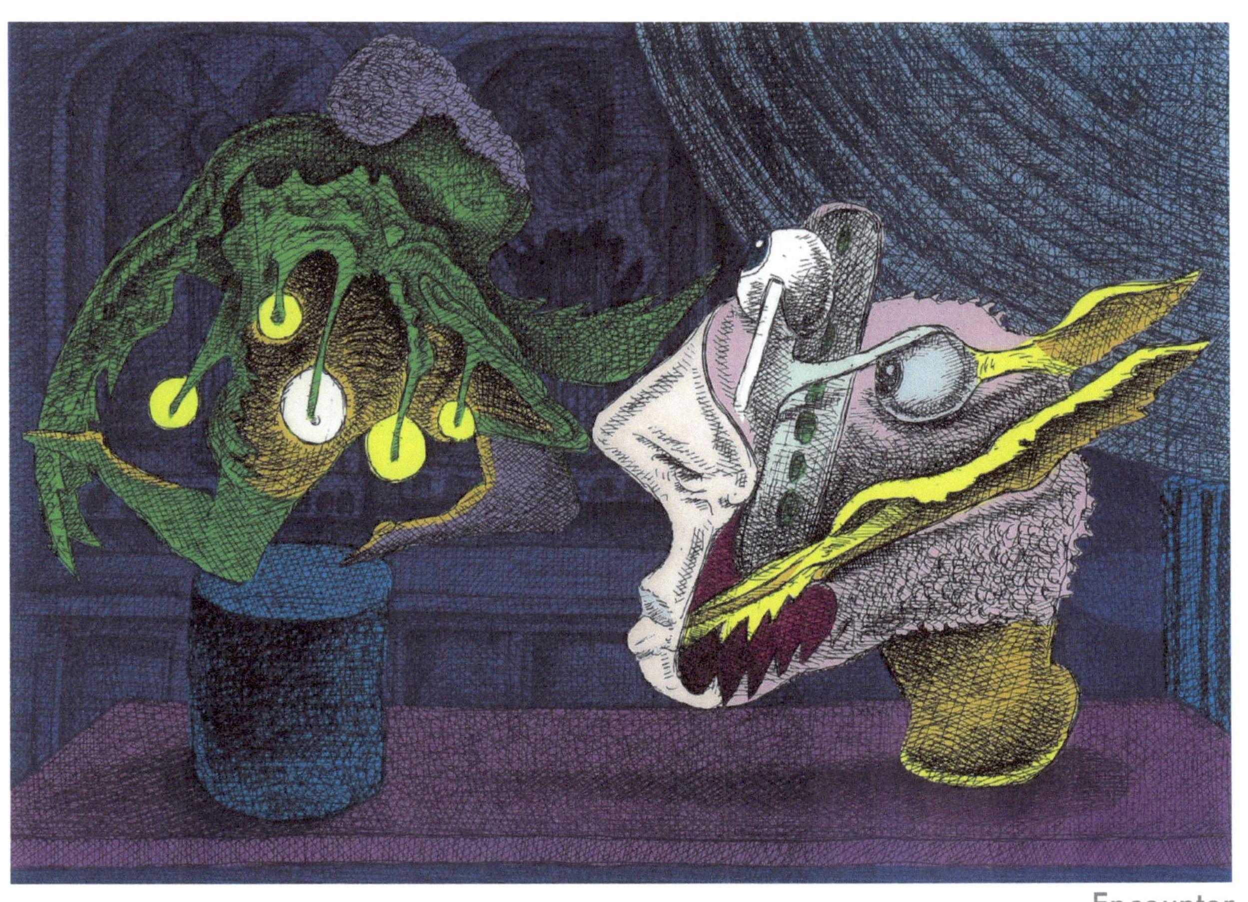

Encounter

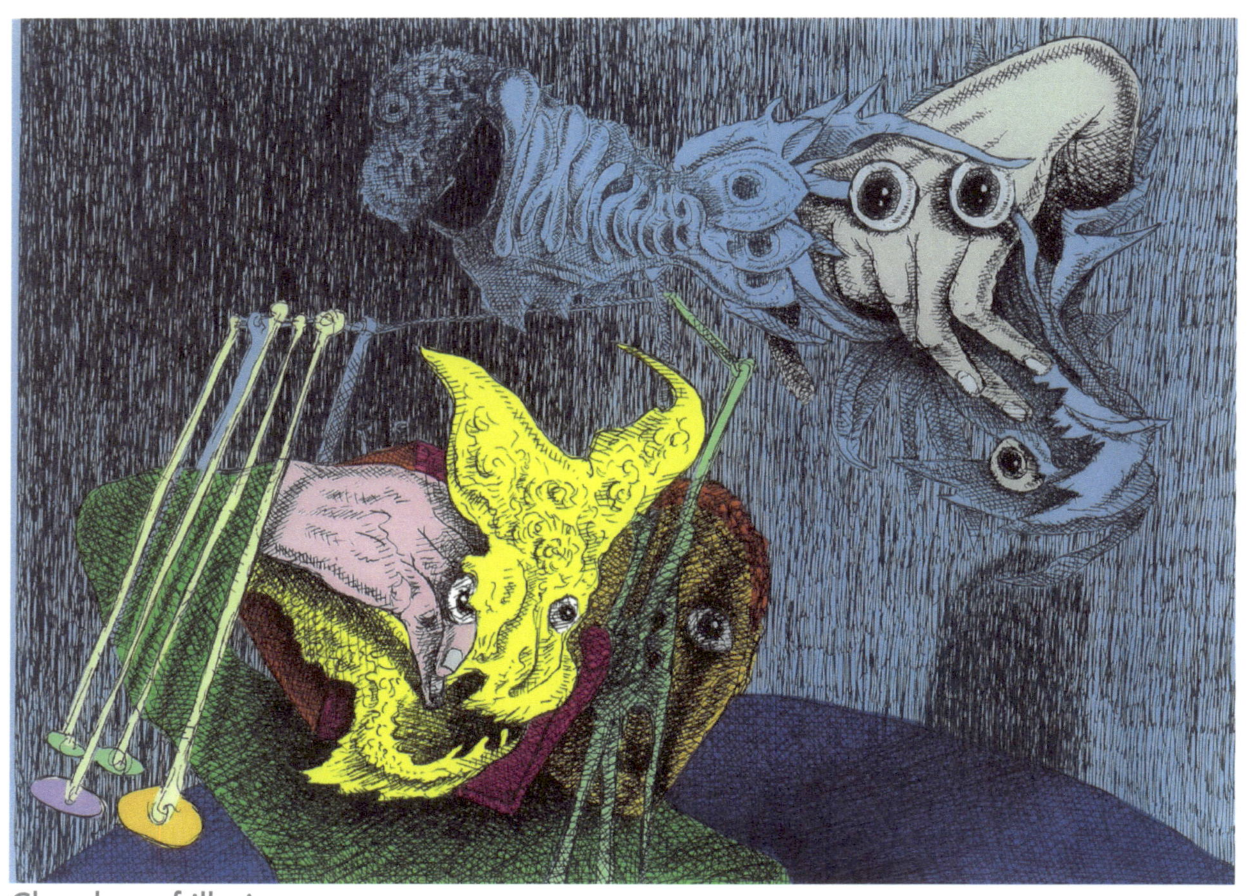

Chamber of illusions

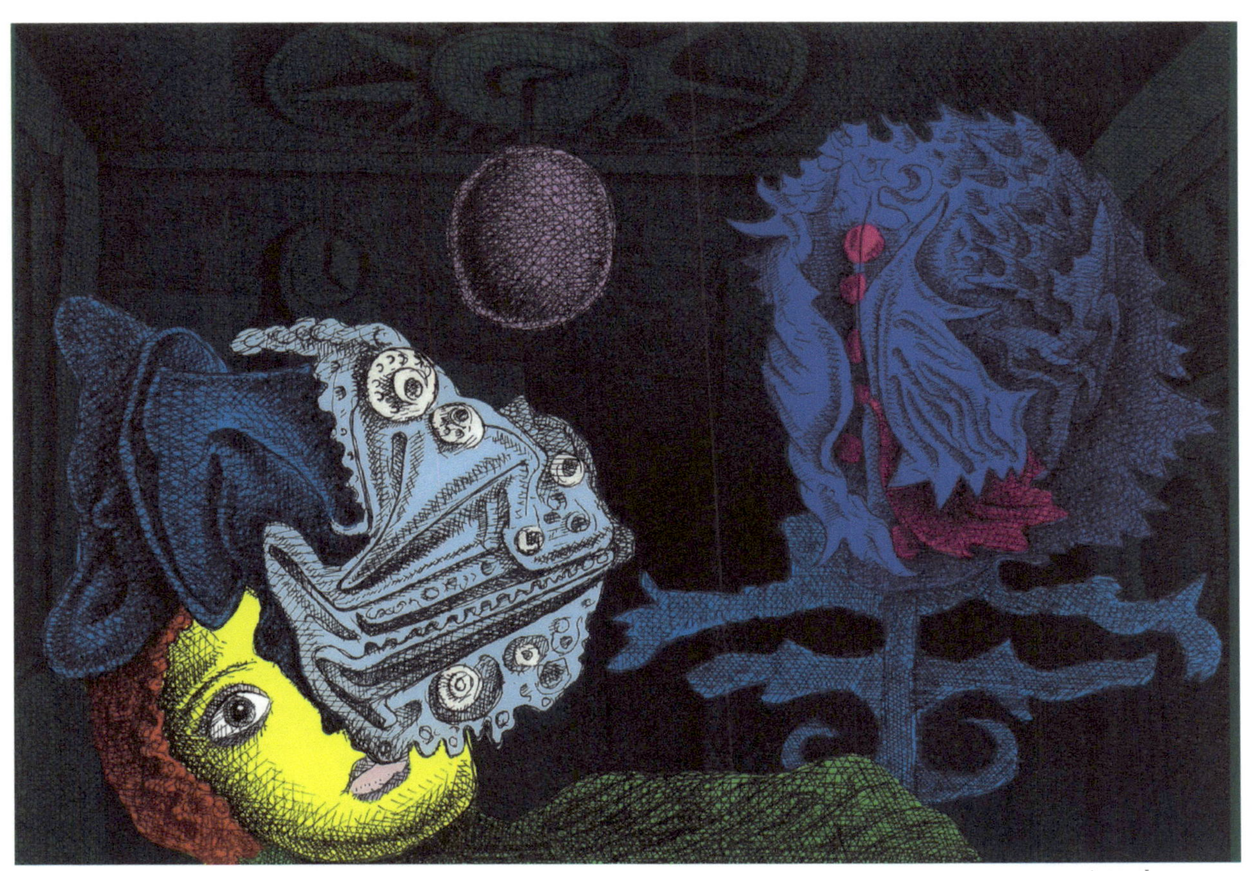

Nightmare

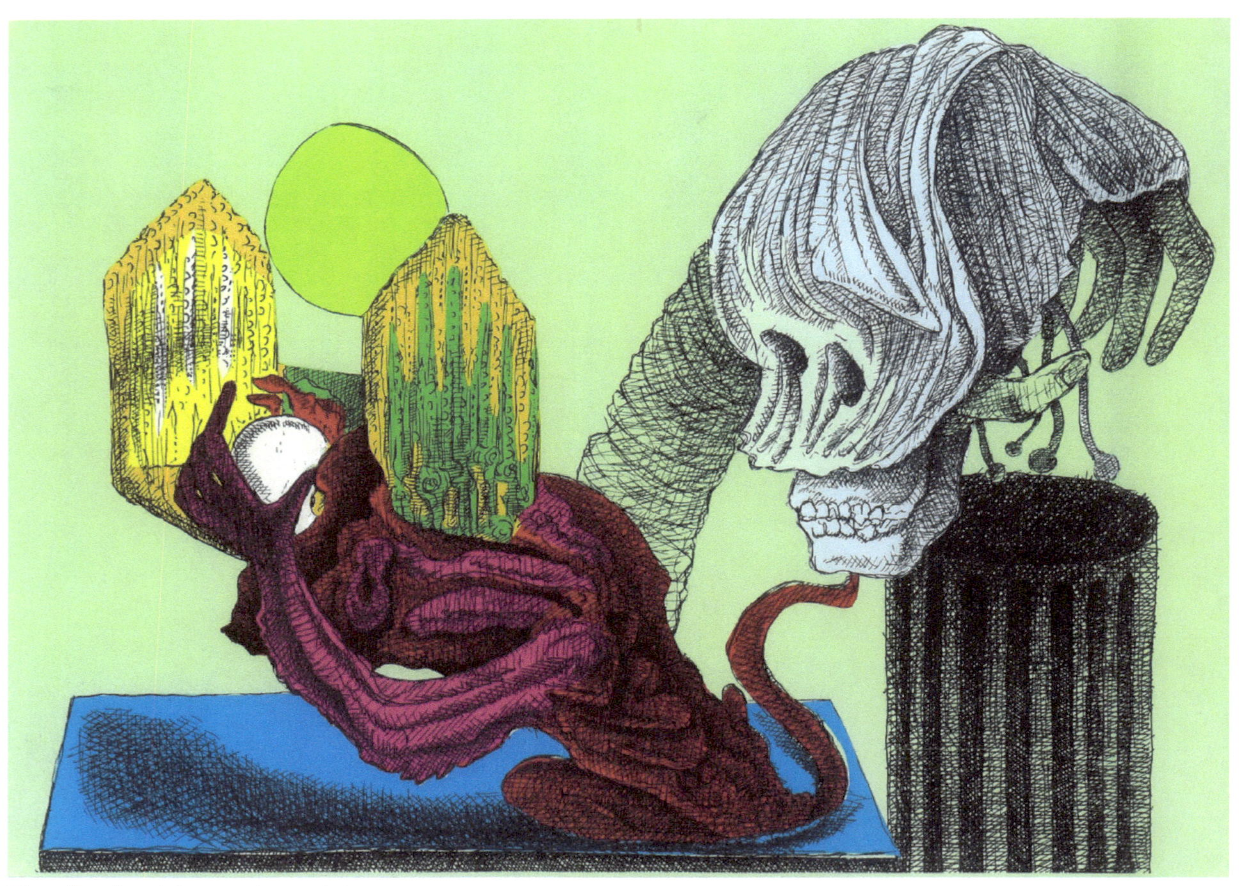

The fool with a wise vision

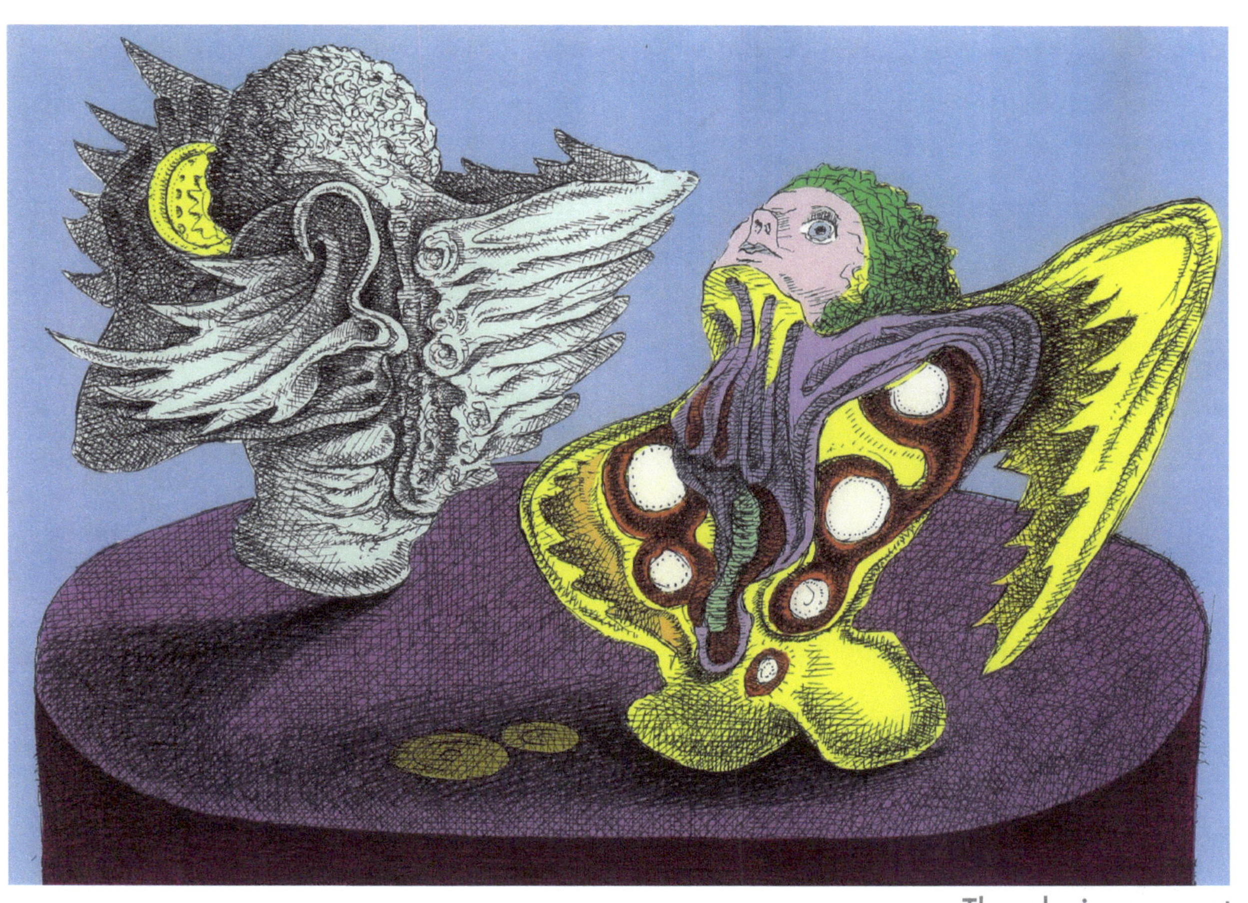

The glorious secret

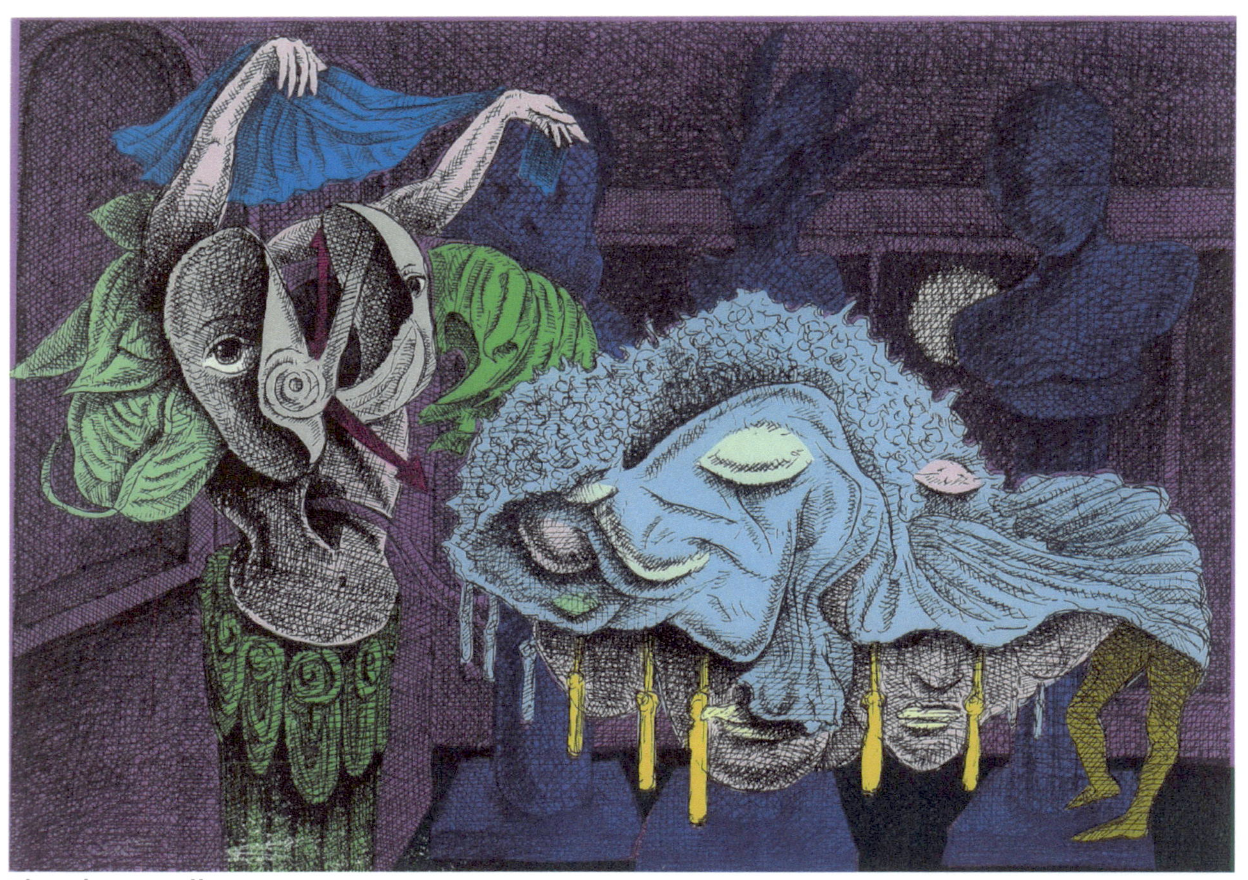

The sleepwalker

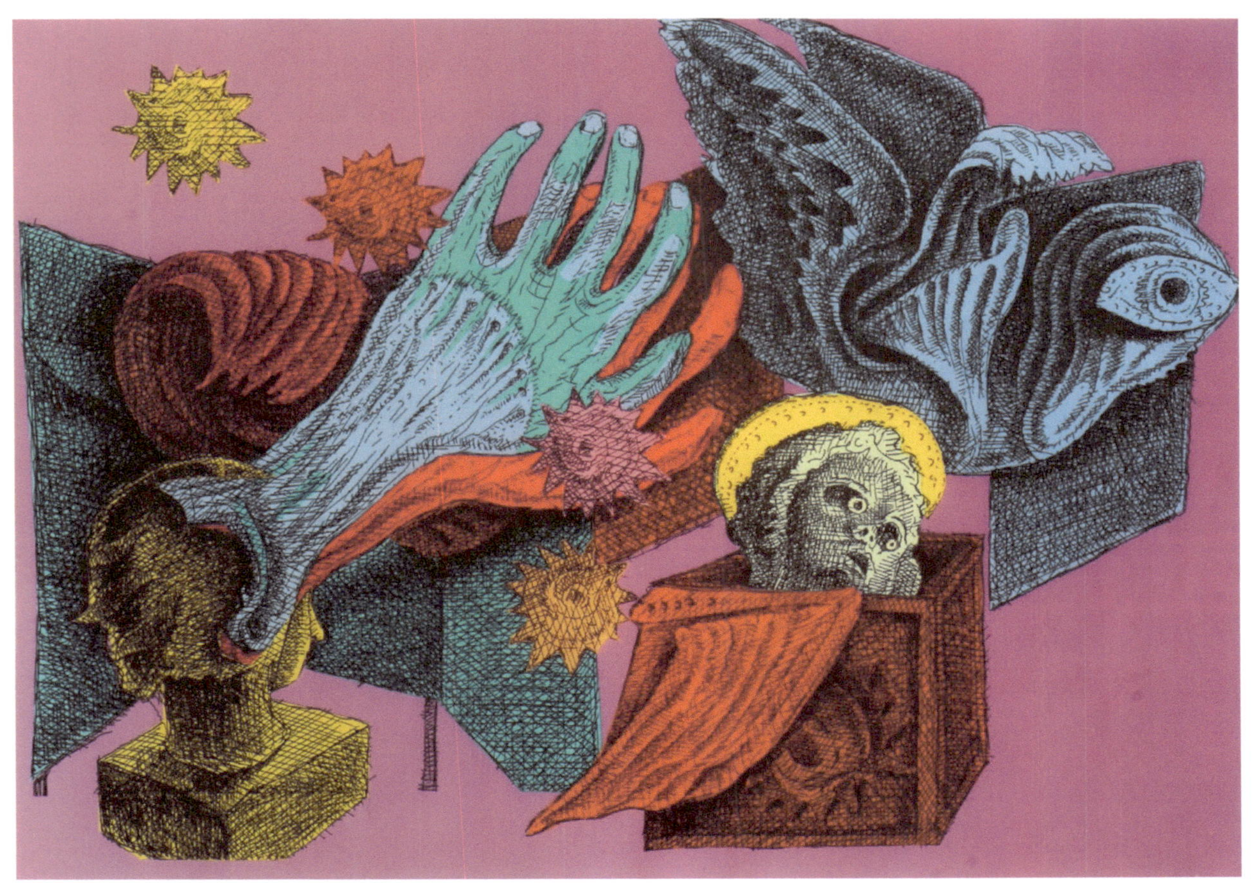

Poet

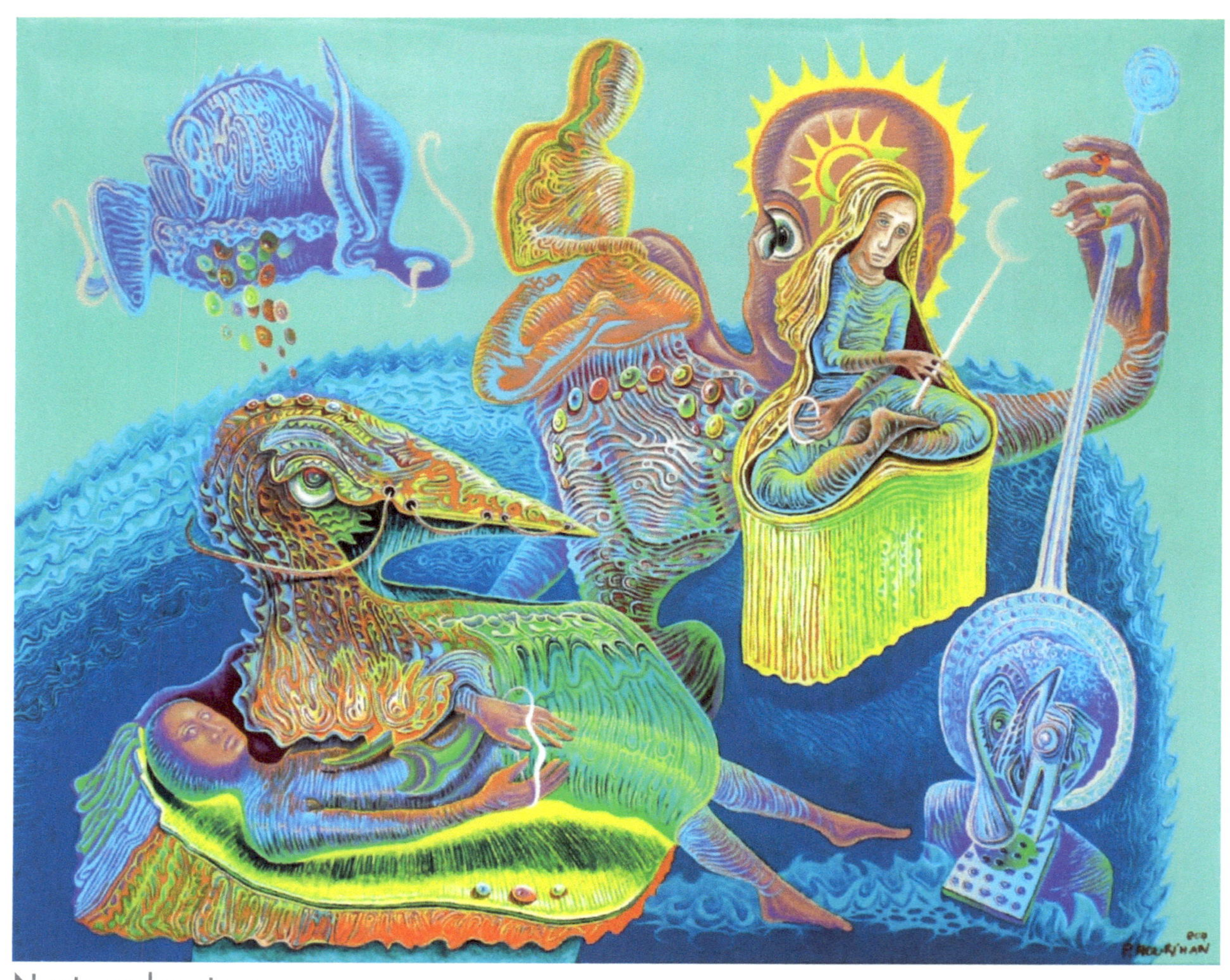

Nocturnal waters

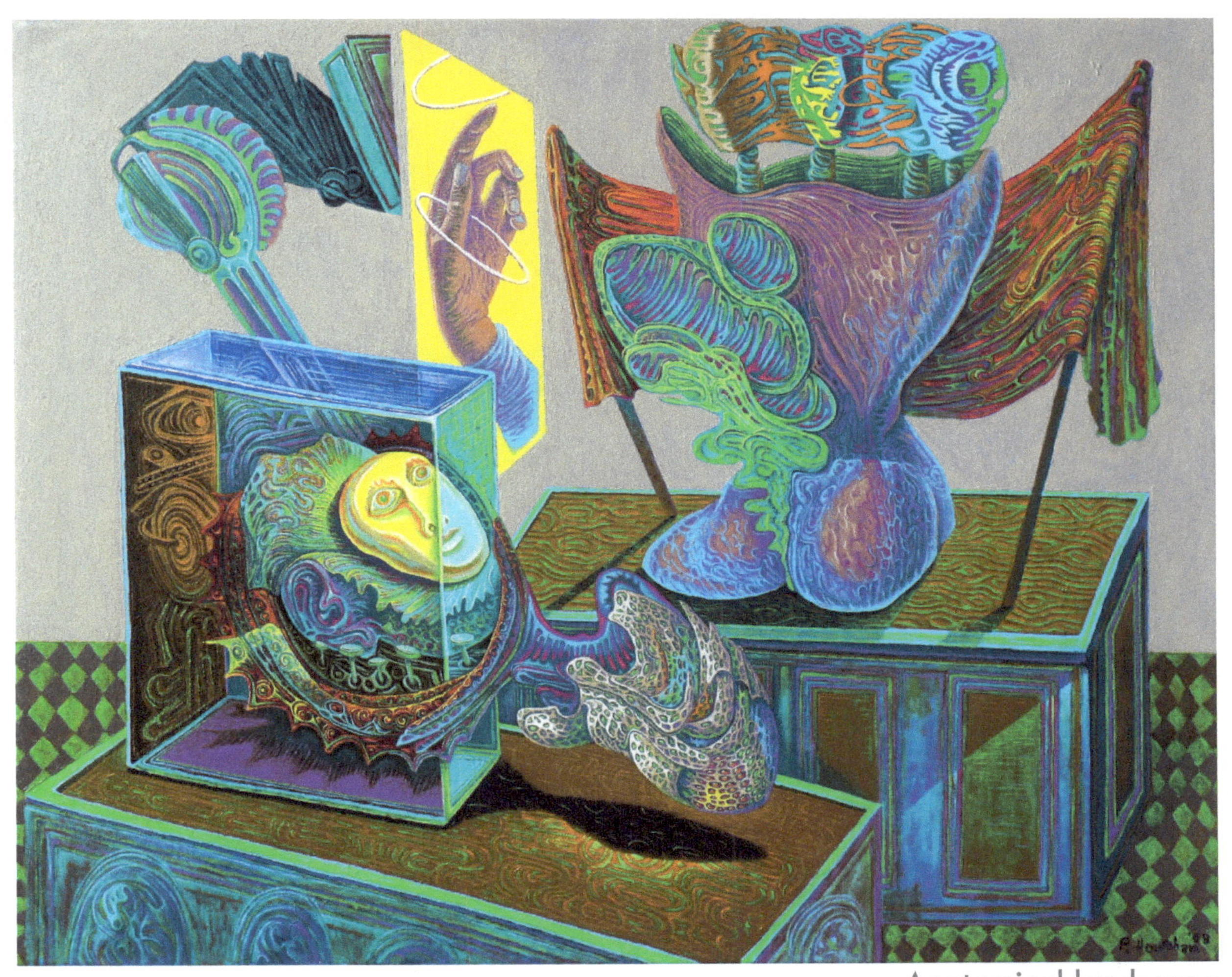

Anatomical landscape

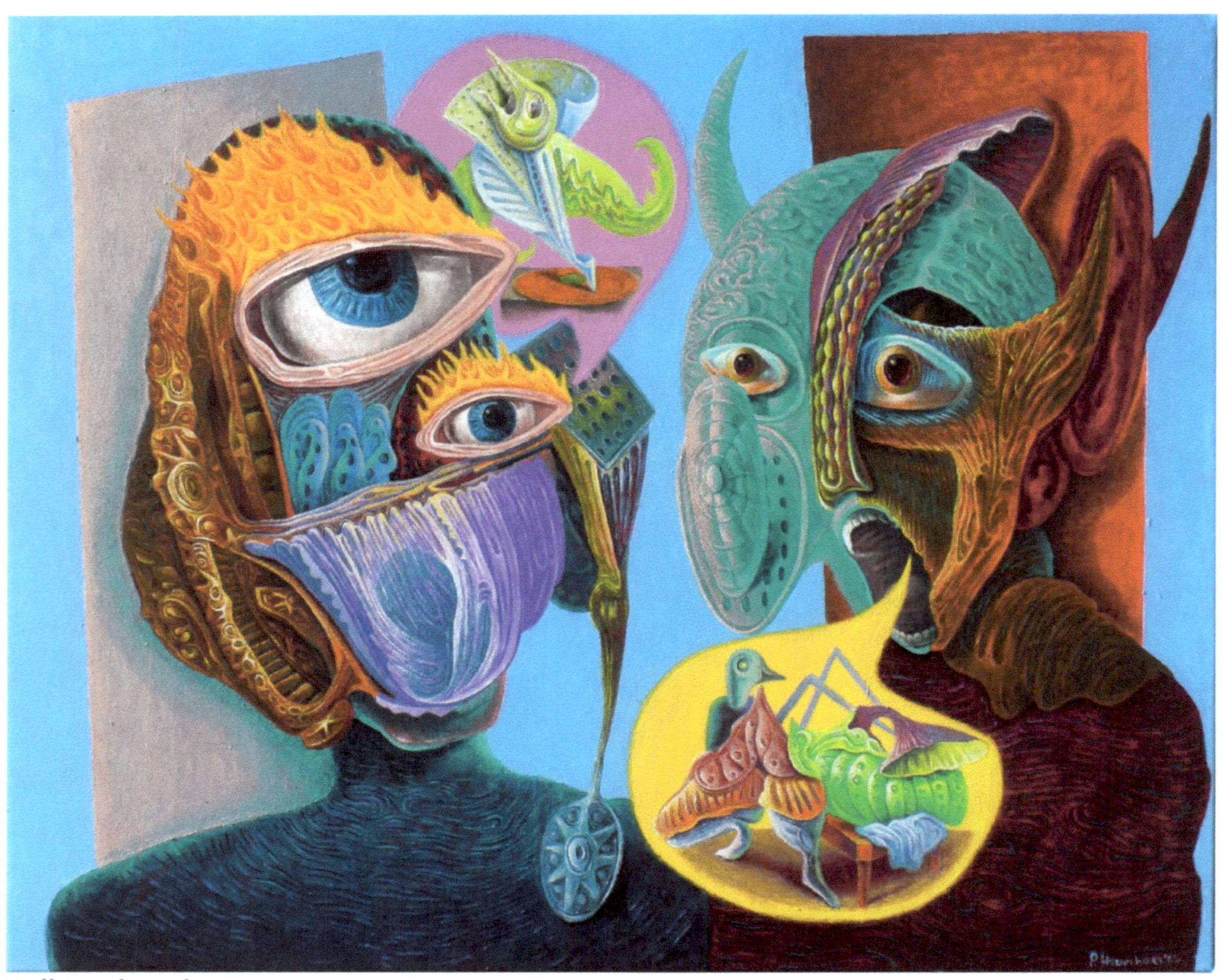

Talking heads

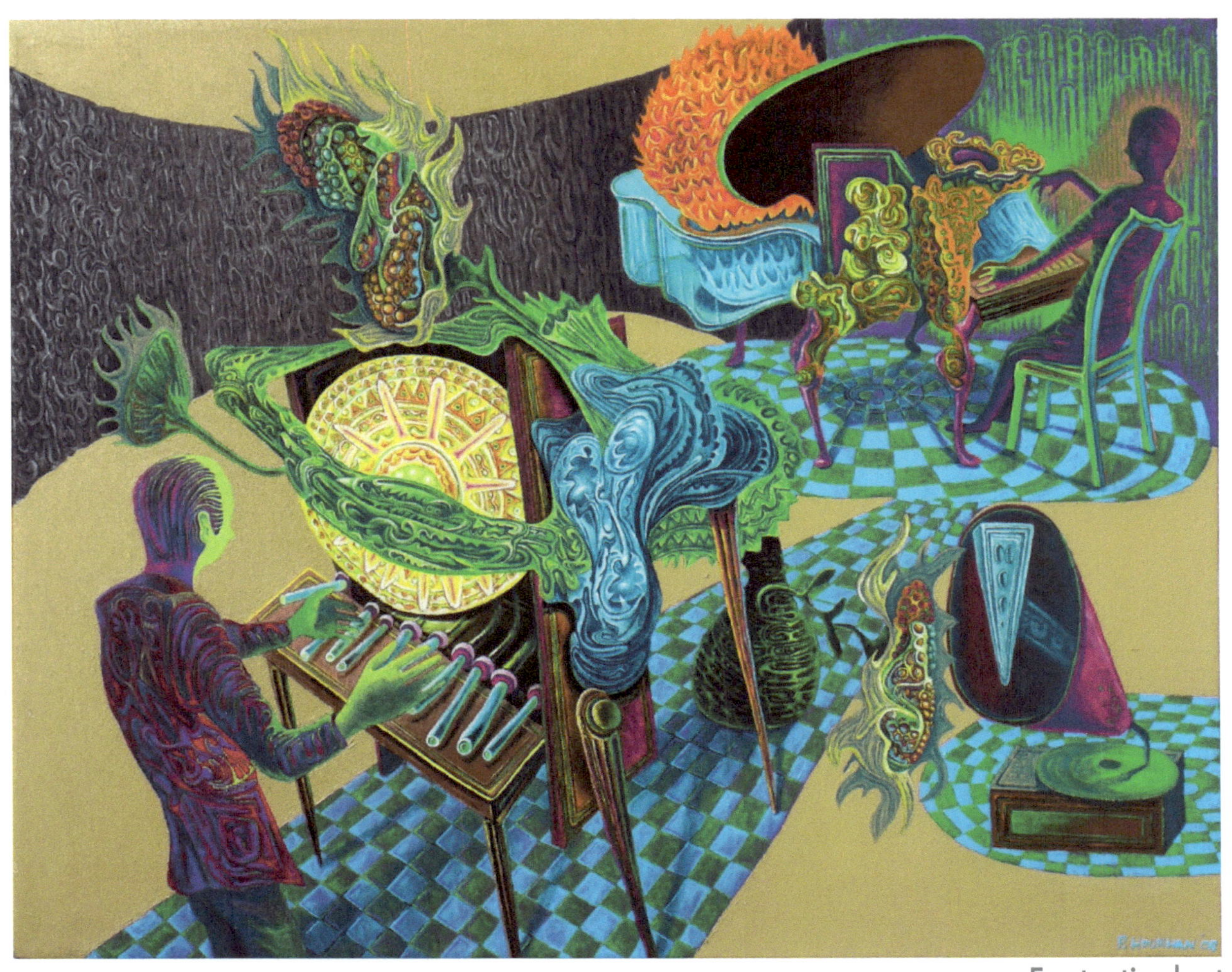

Fantastic duet

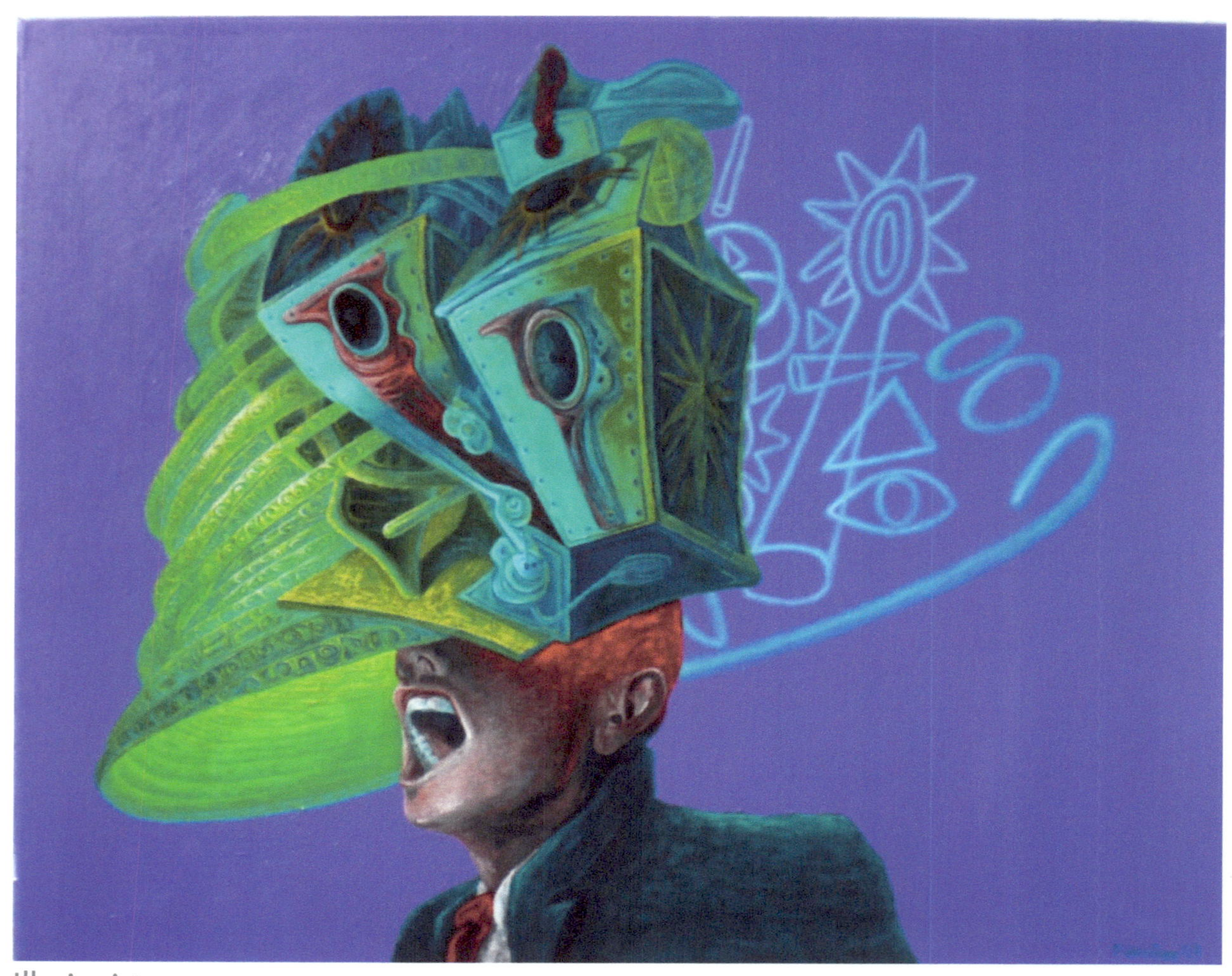

Illusionist

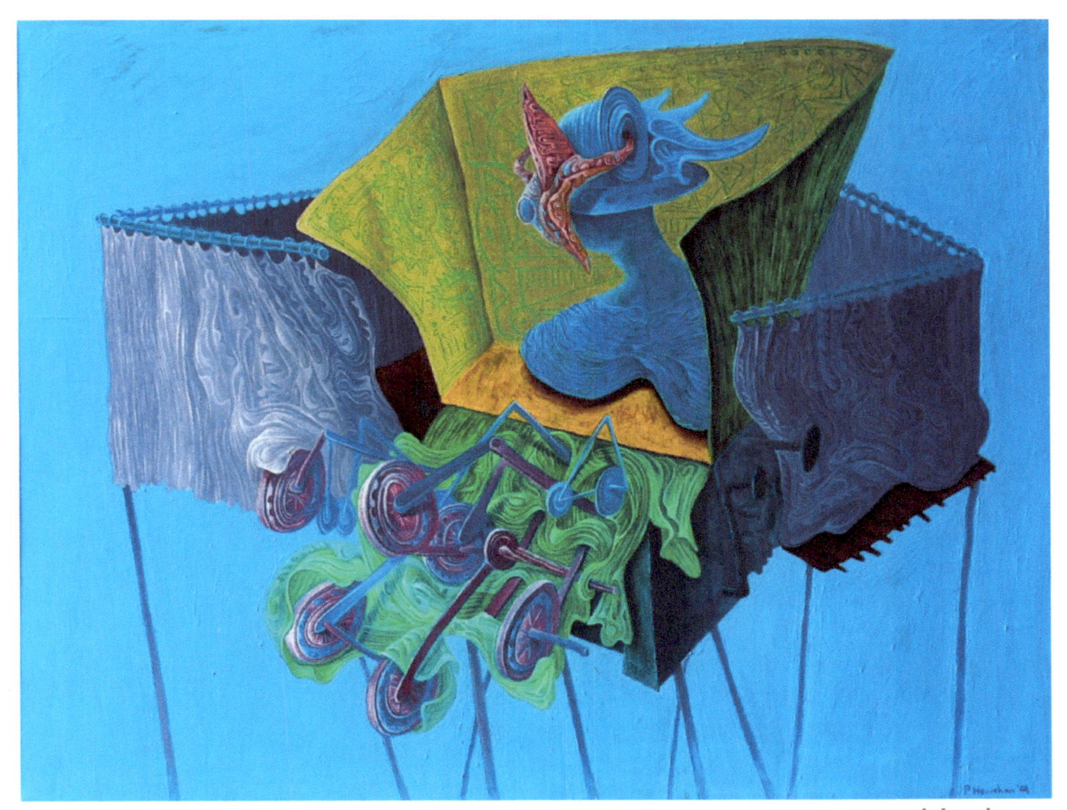

Seeing blindness

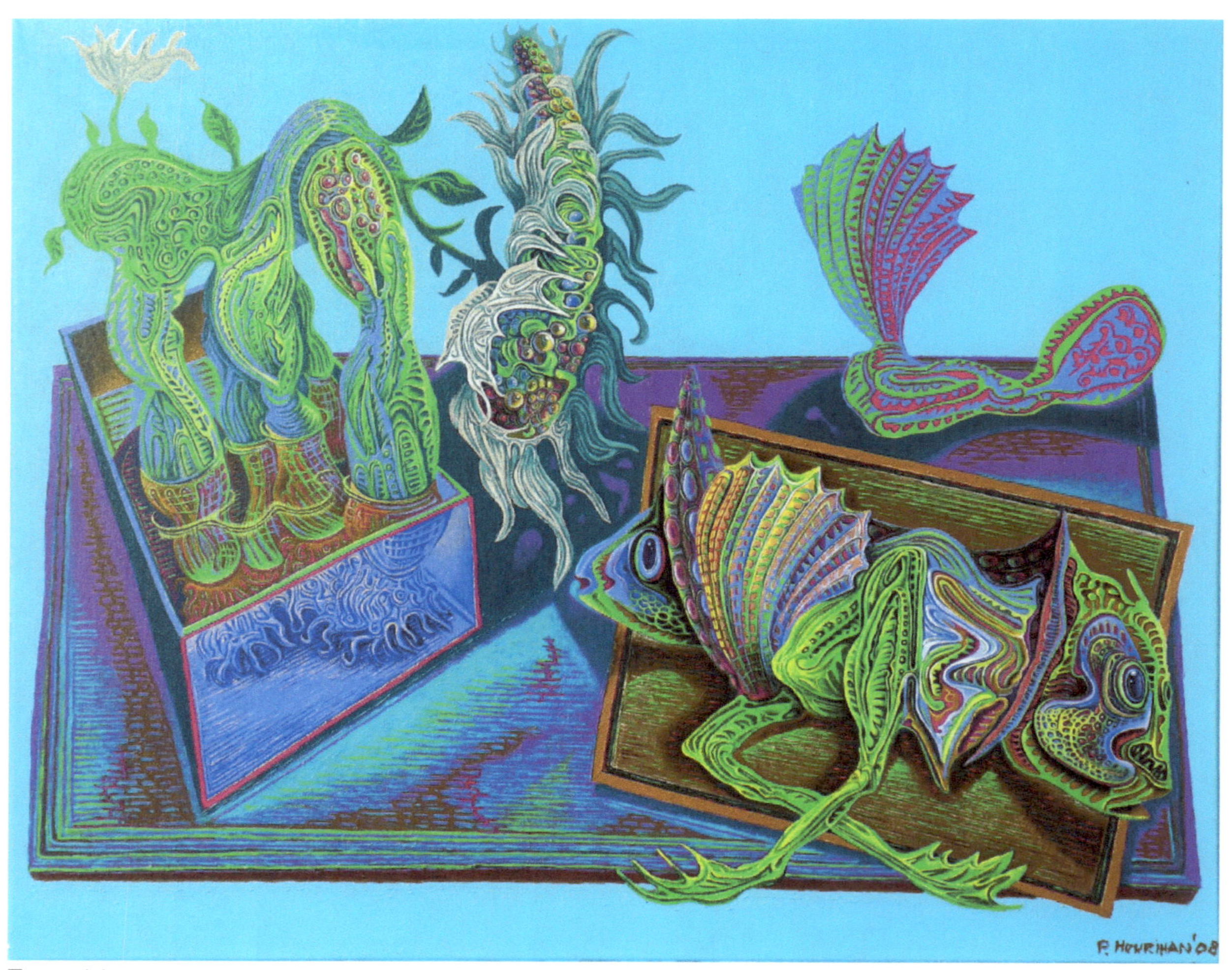

Transition

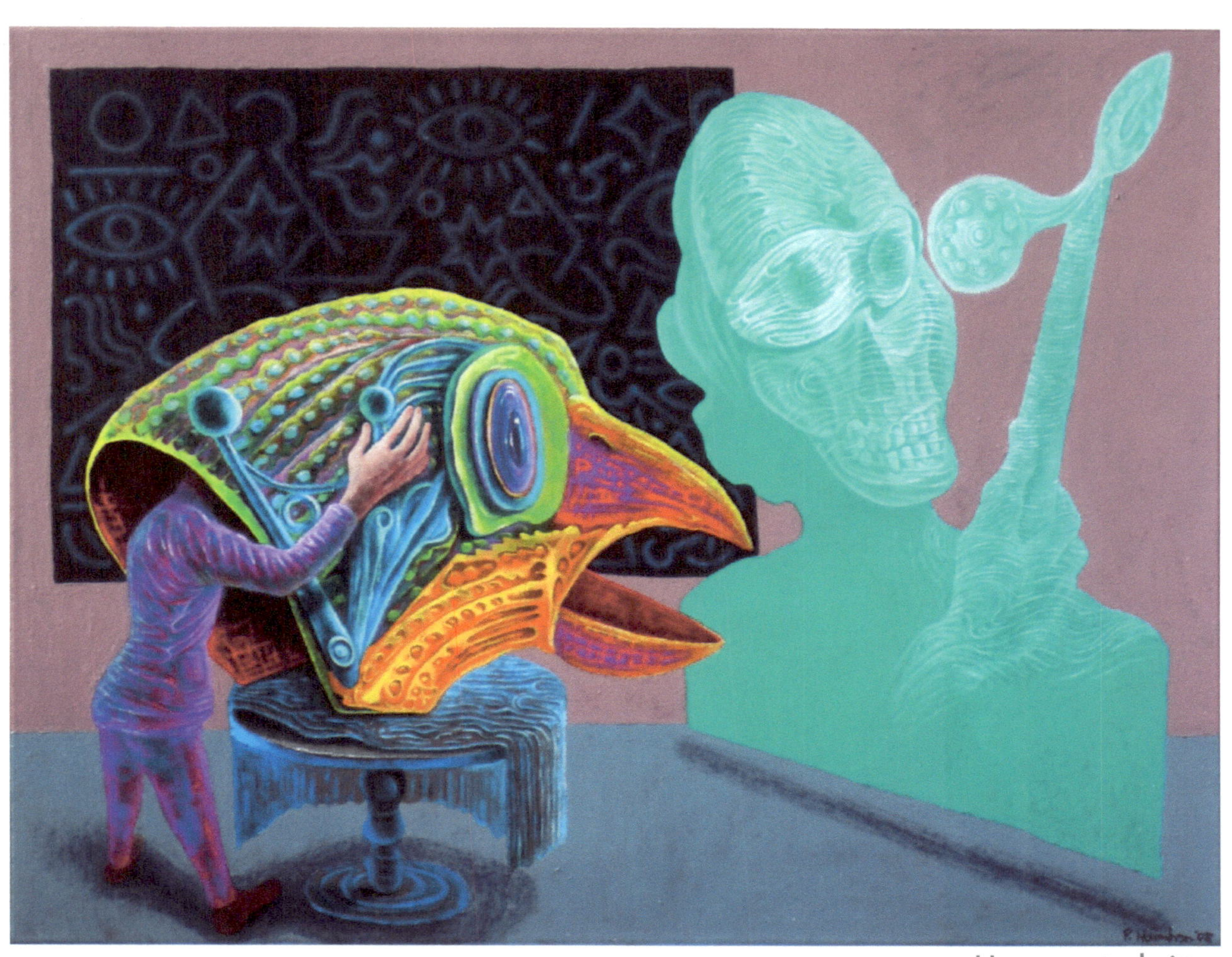

Unexpected sitter

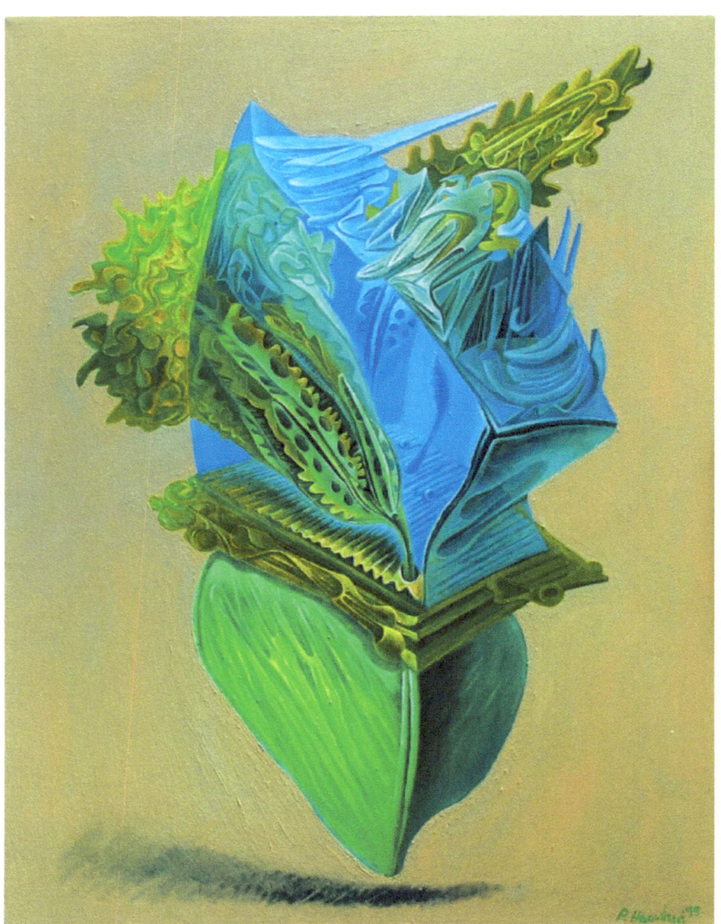
Pod

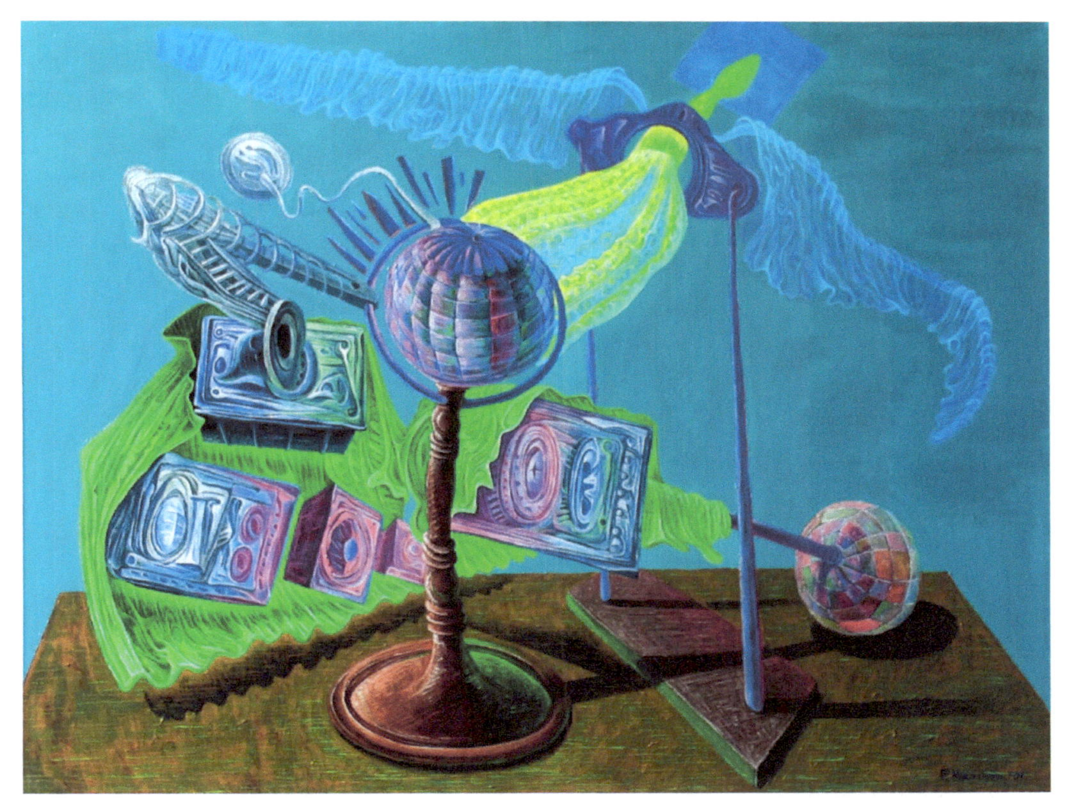

Psychic machine

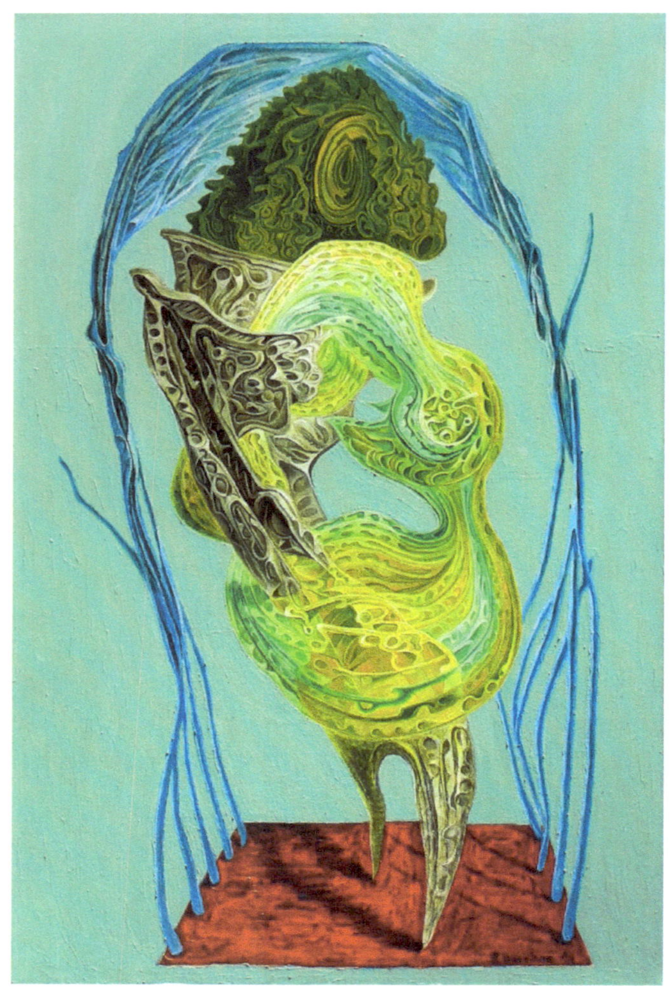

Dancer

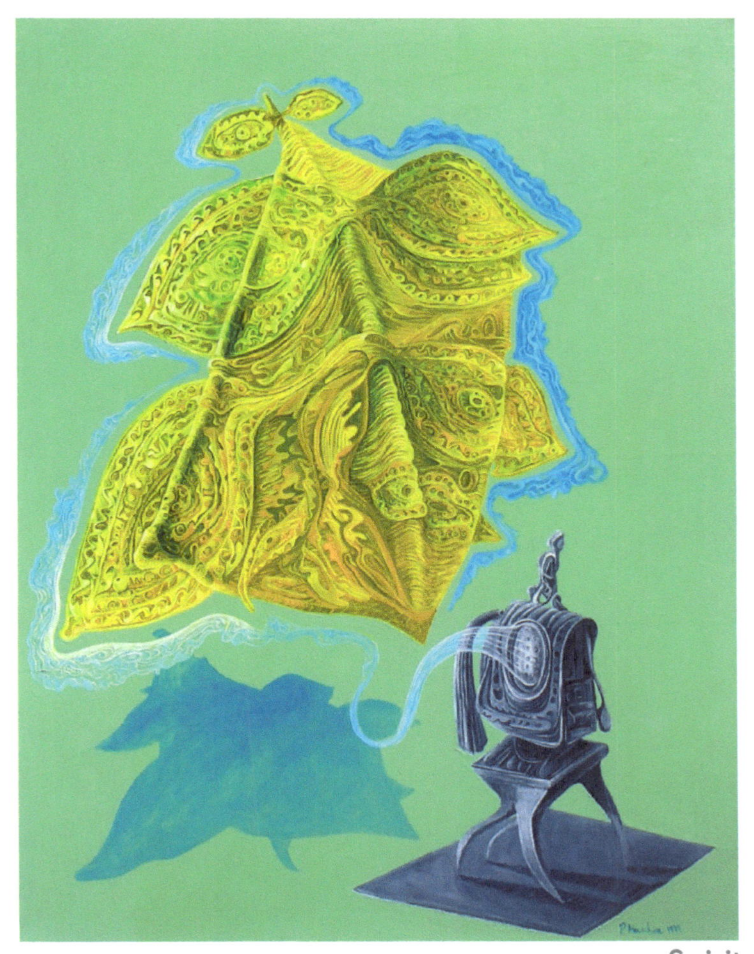

Spirit

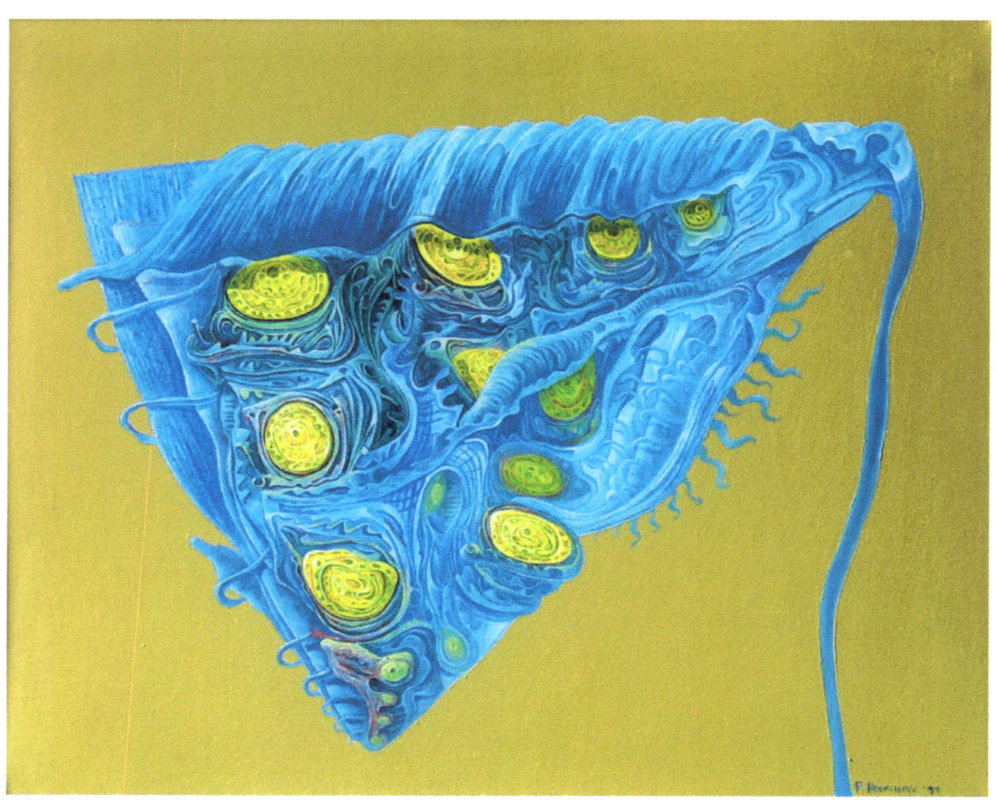
Strange fruit

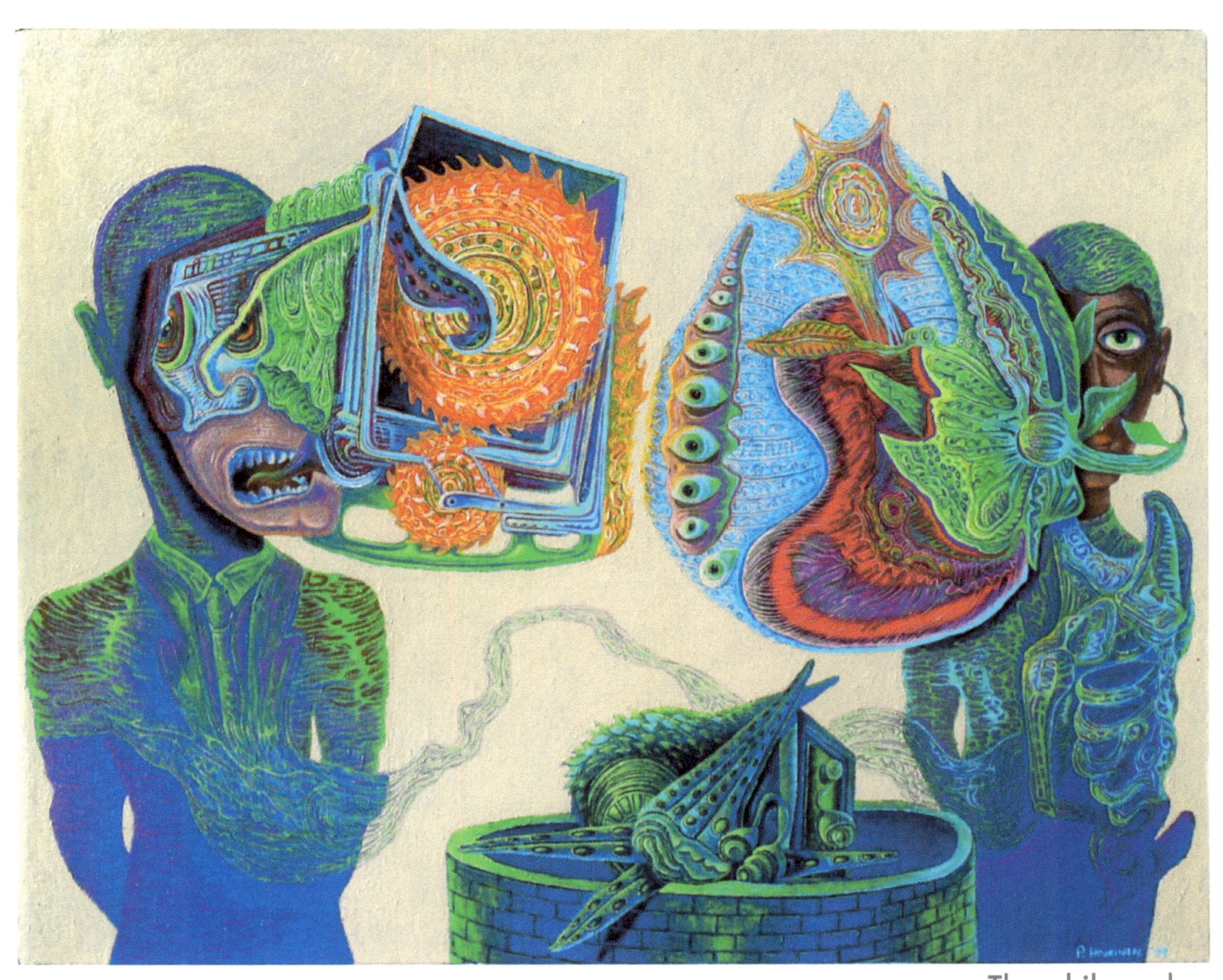

The philosopher

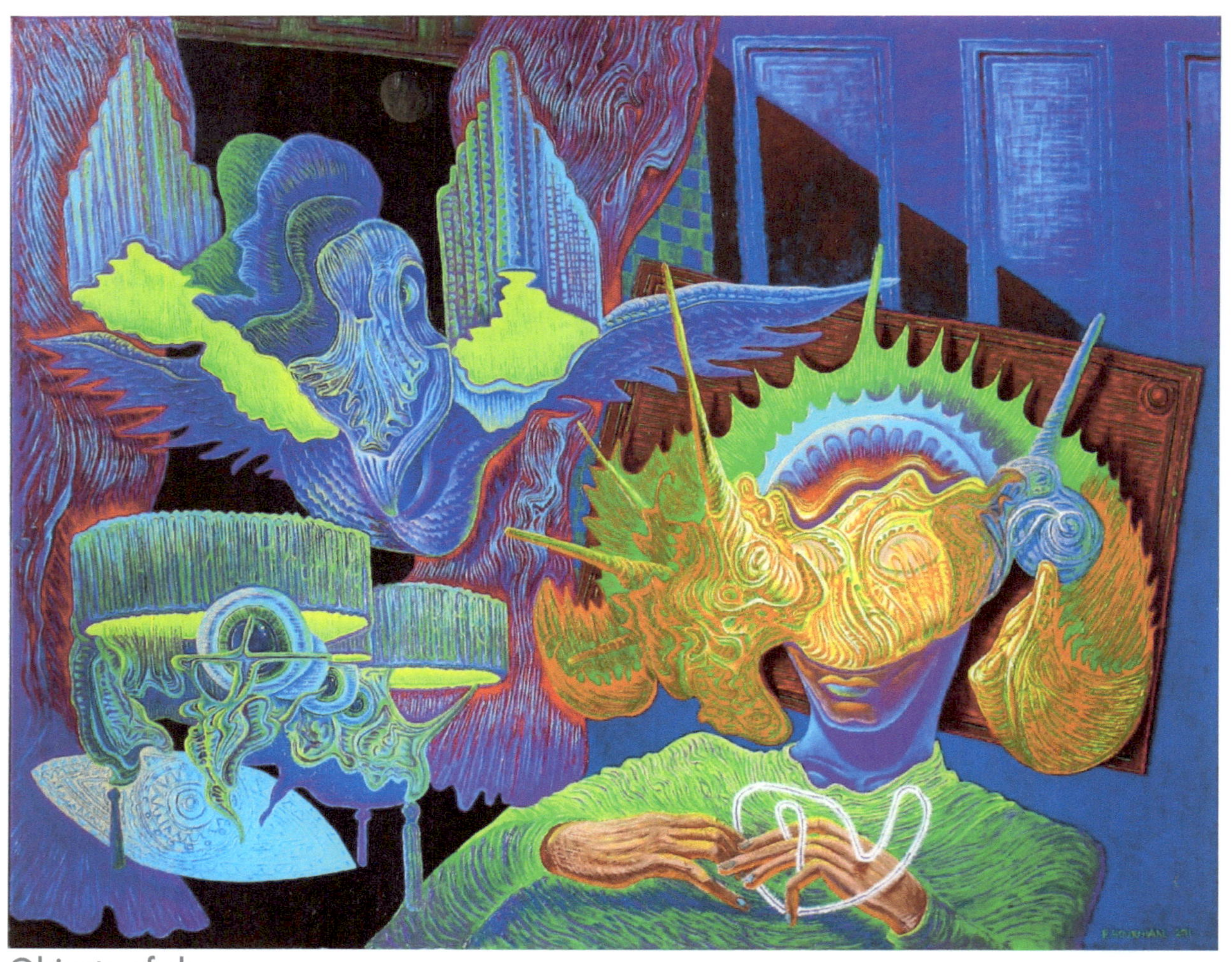
Objects of sleep

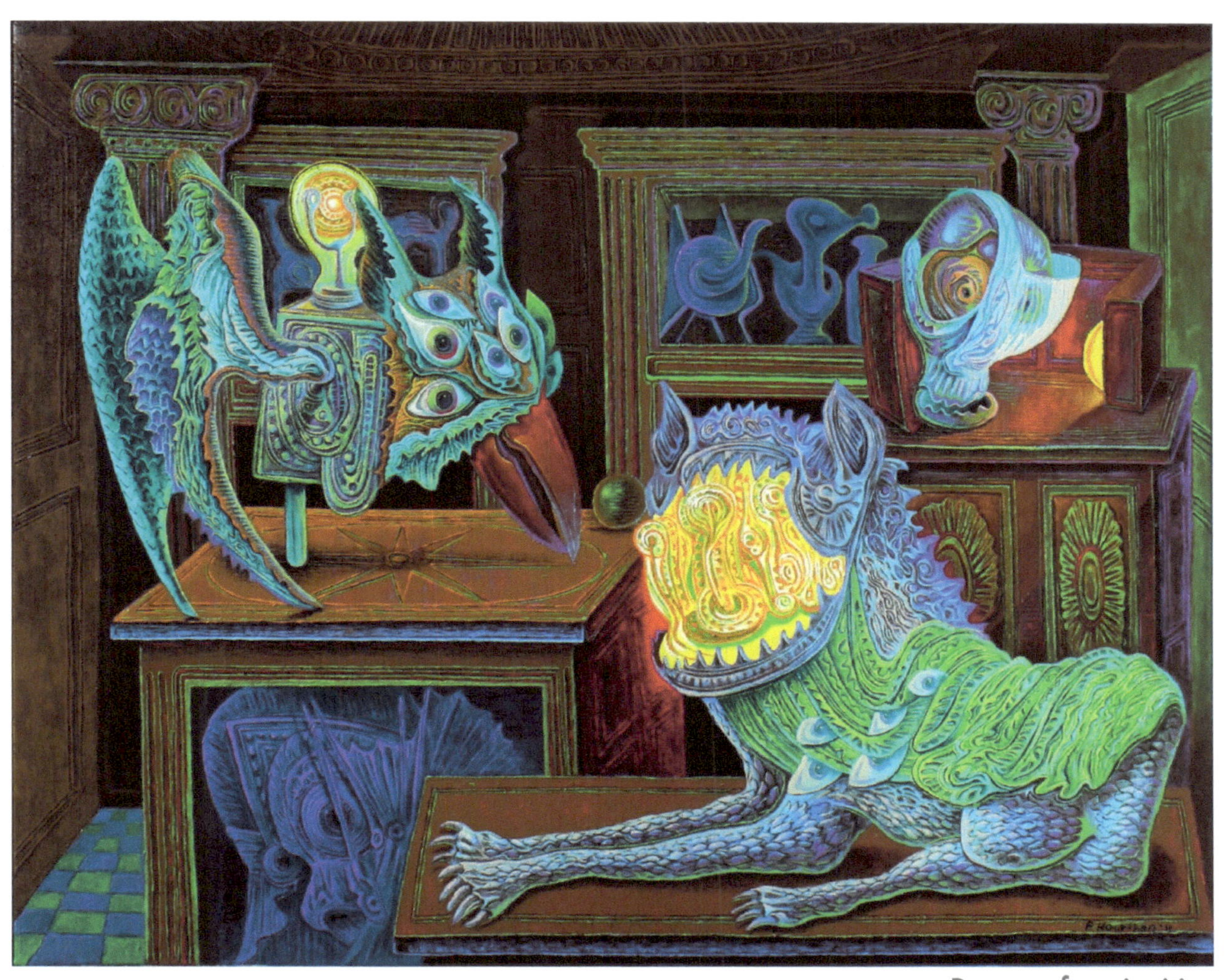

Room of curiosities

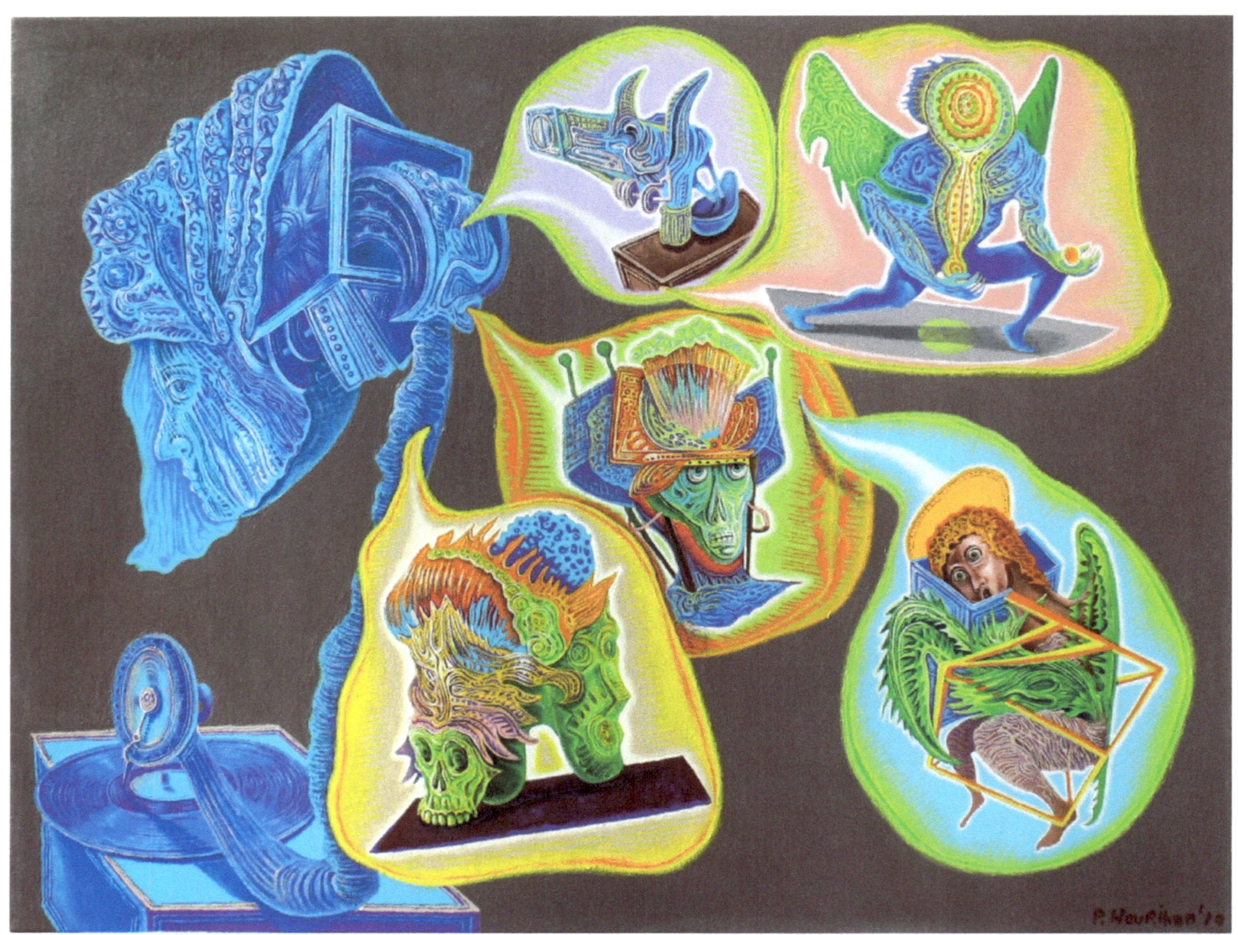

Pandora

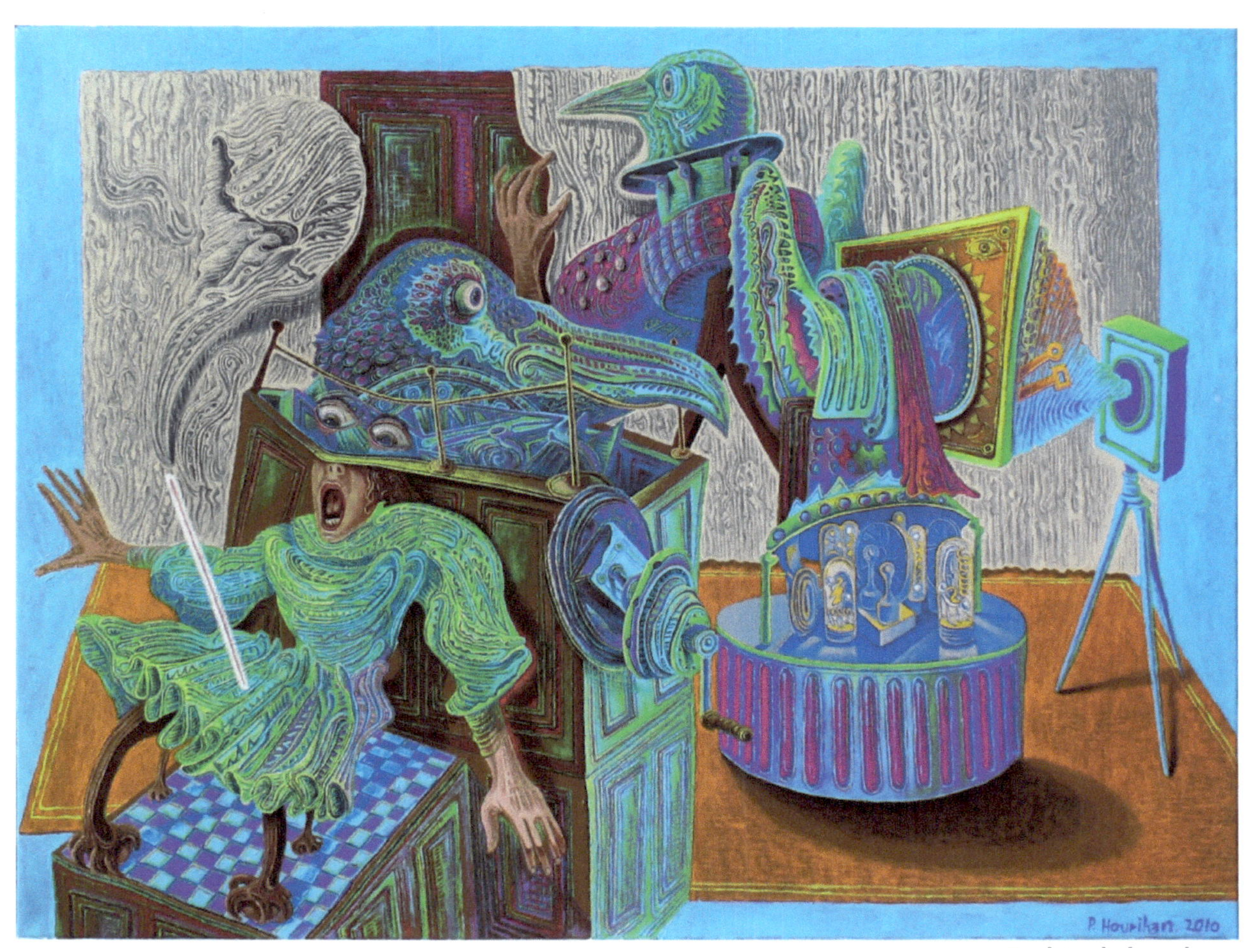

Behind the door

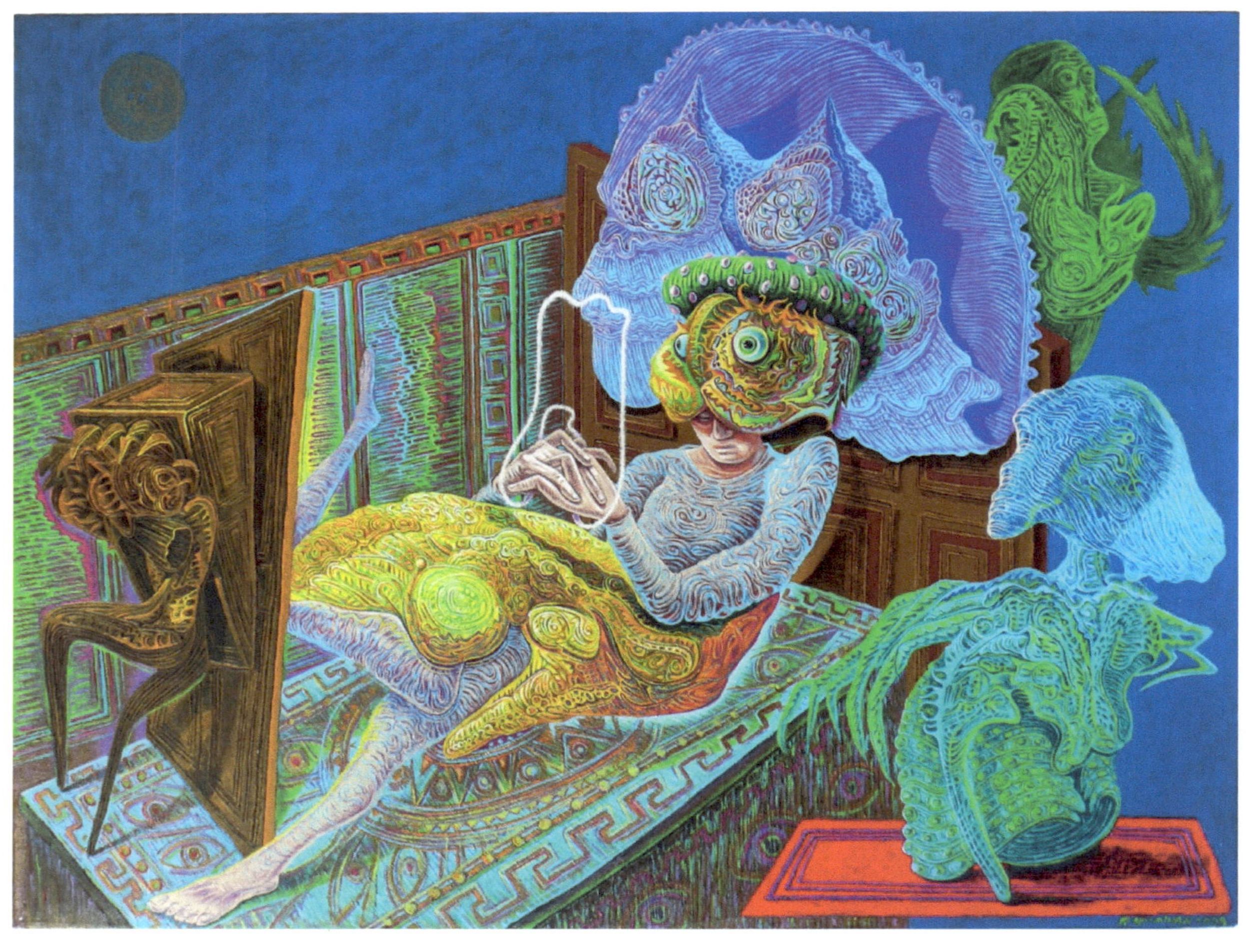

Hypnos

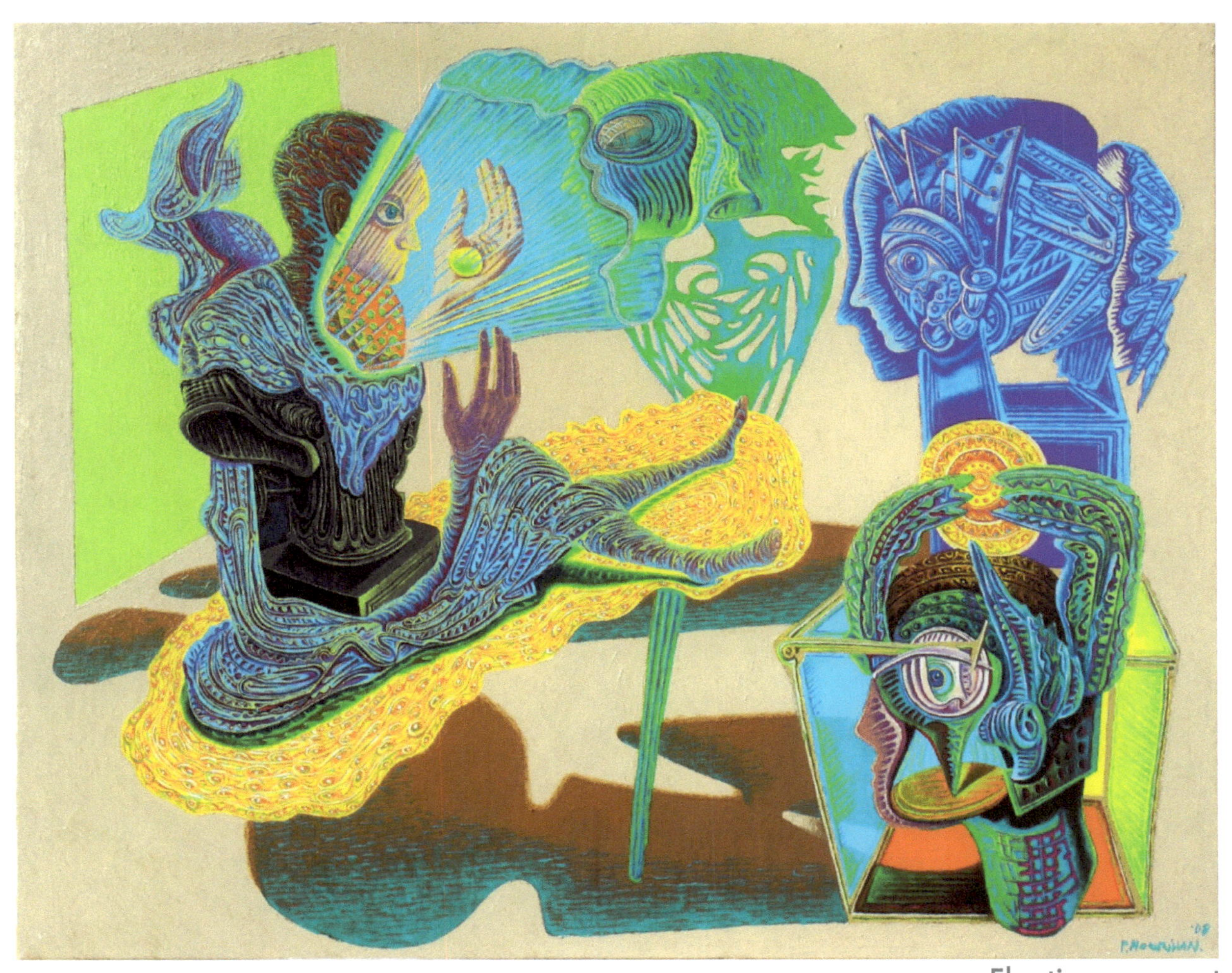

Fleeting moment

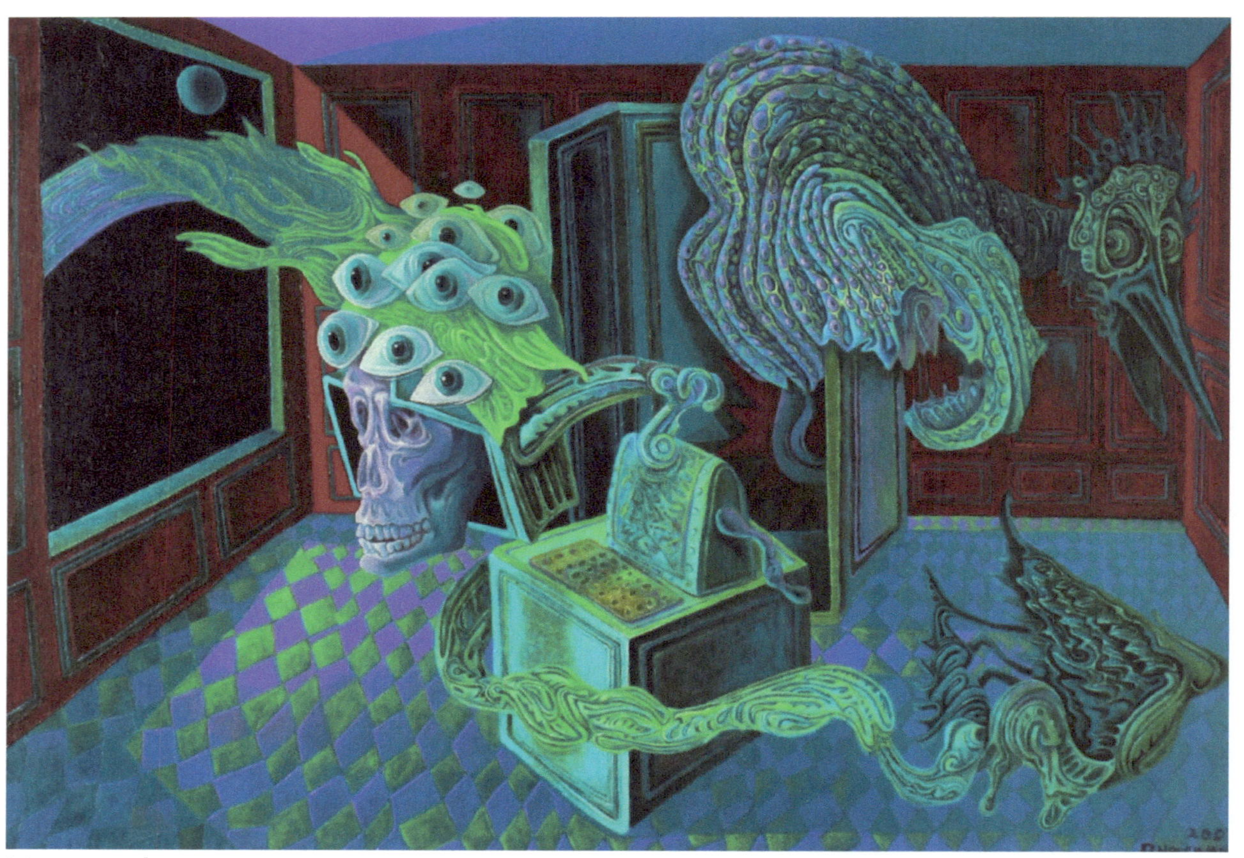

Nocturnal companions

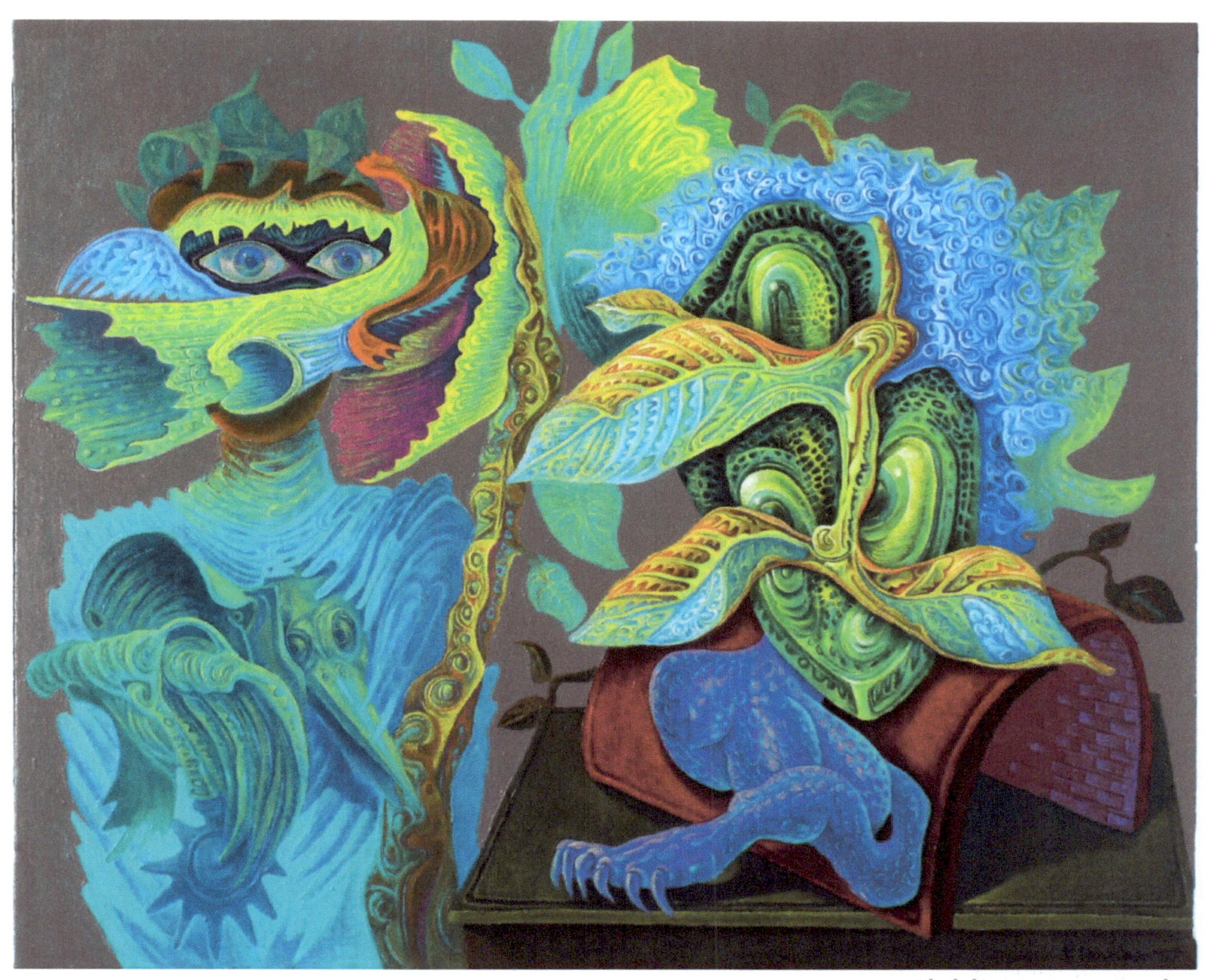

Child's secret garden

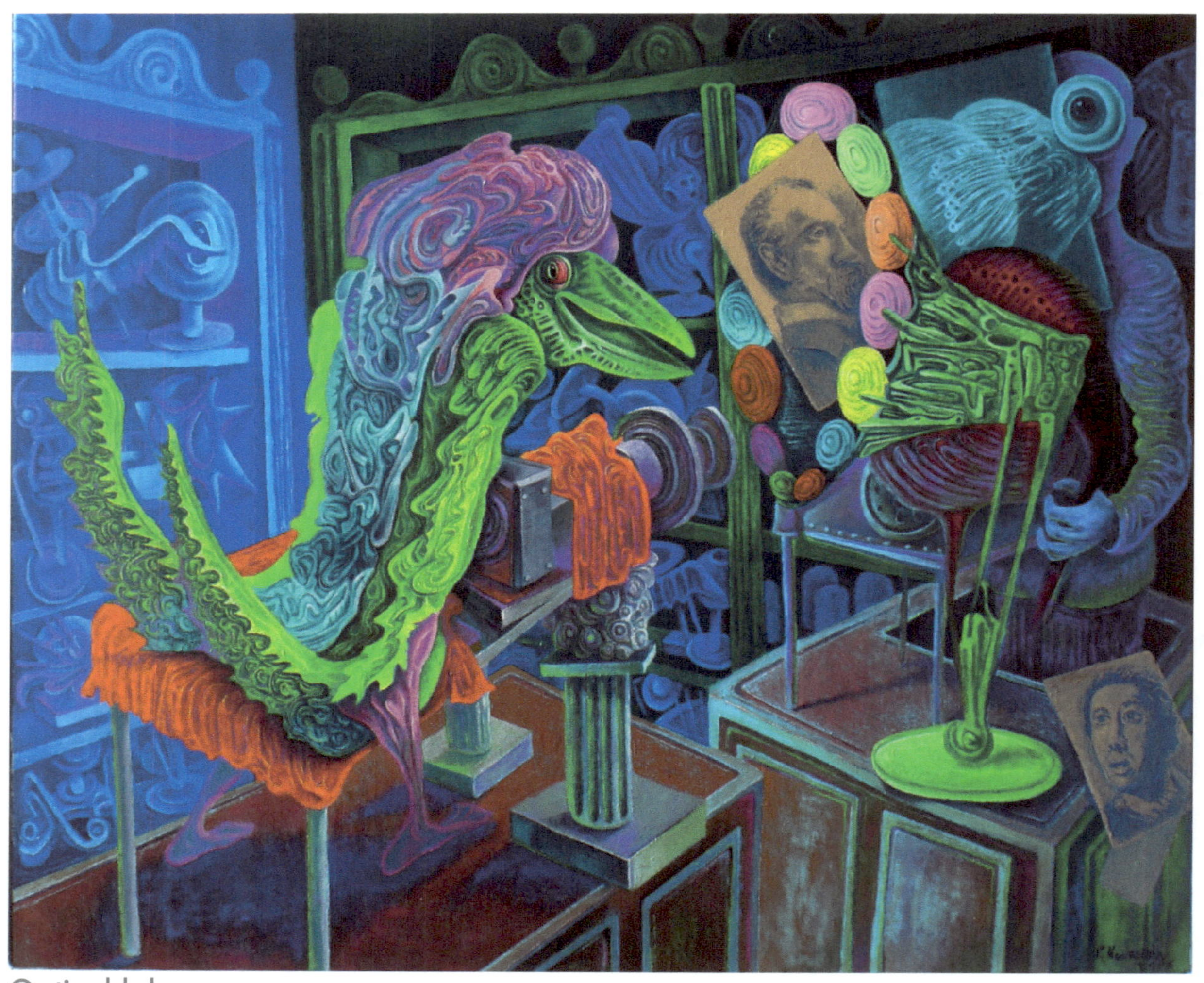
Optical lab

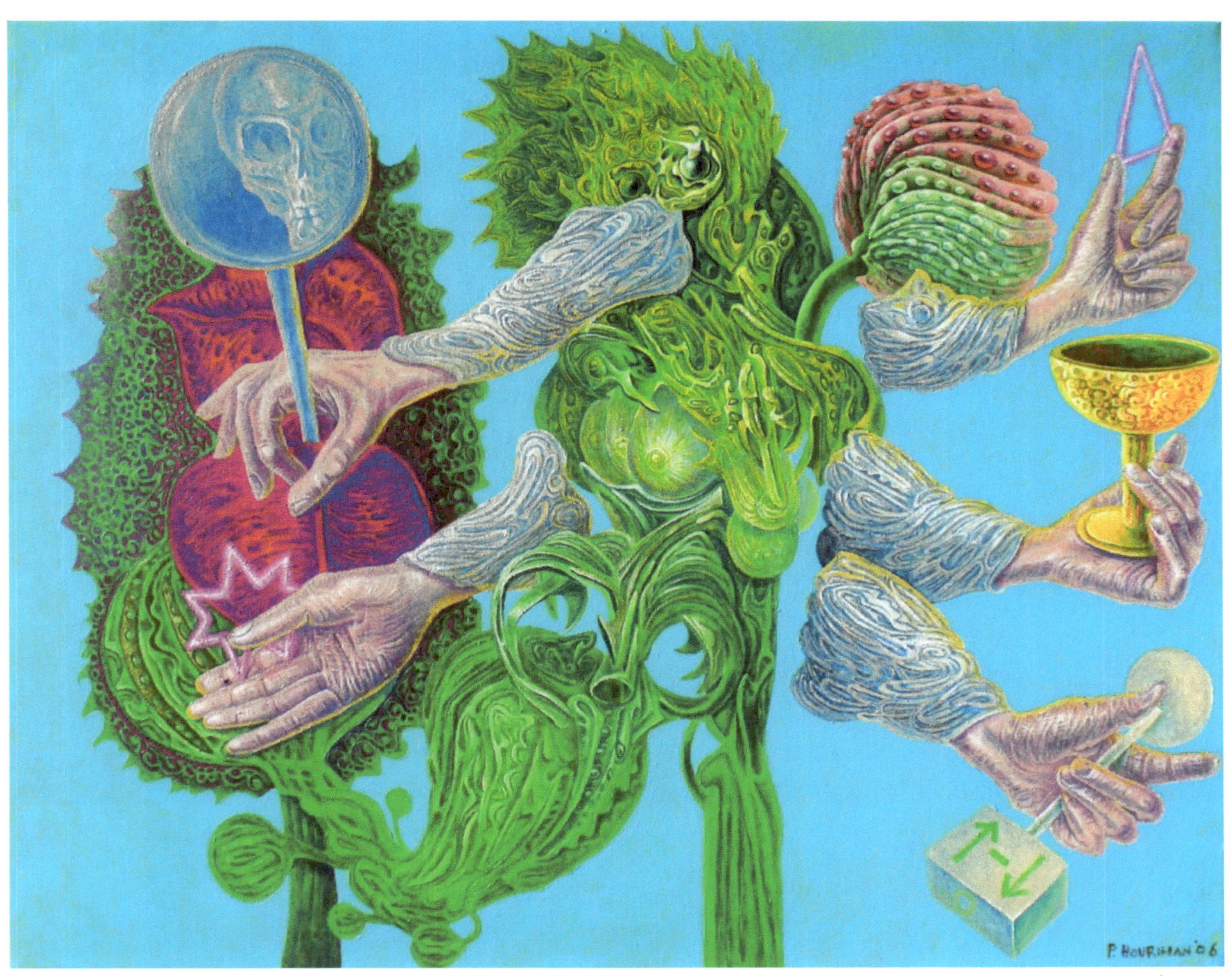

Azna

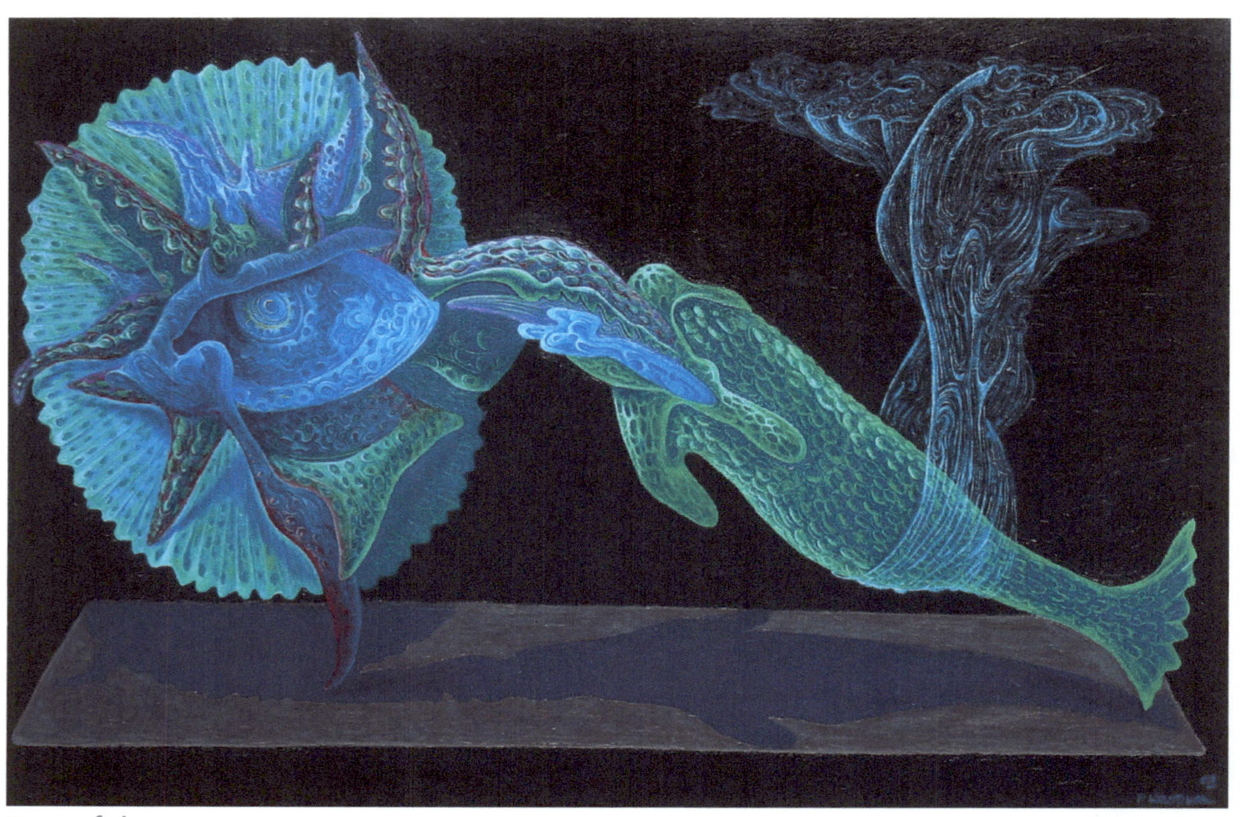

Peaceful eye

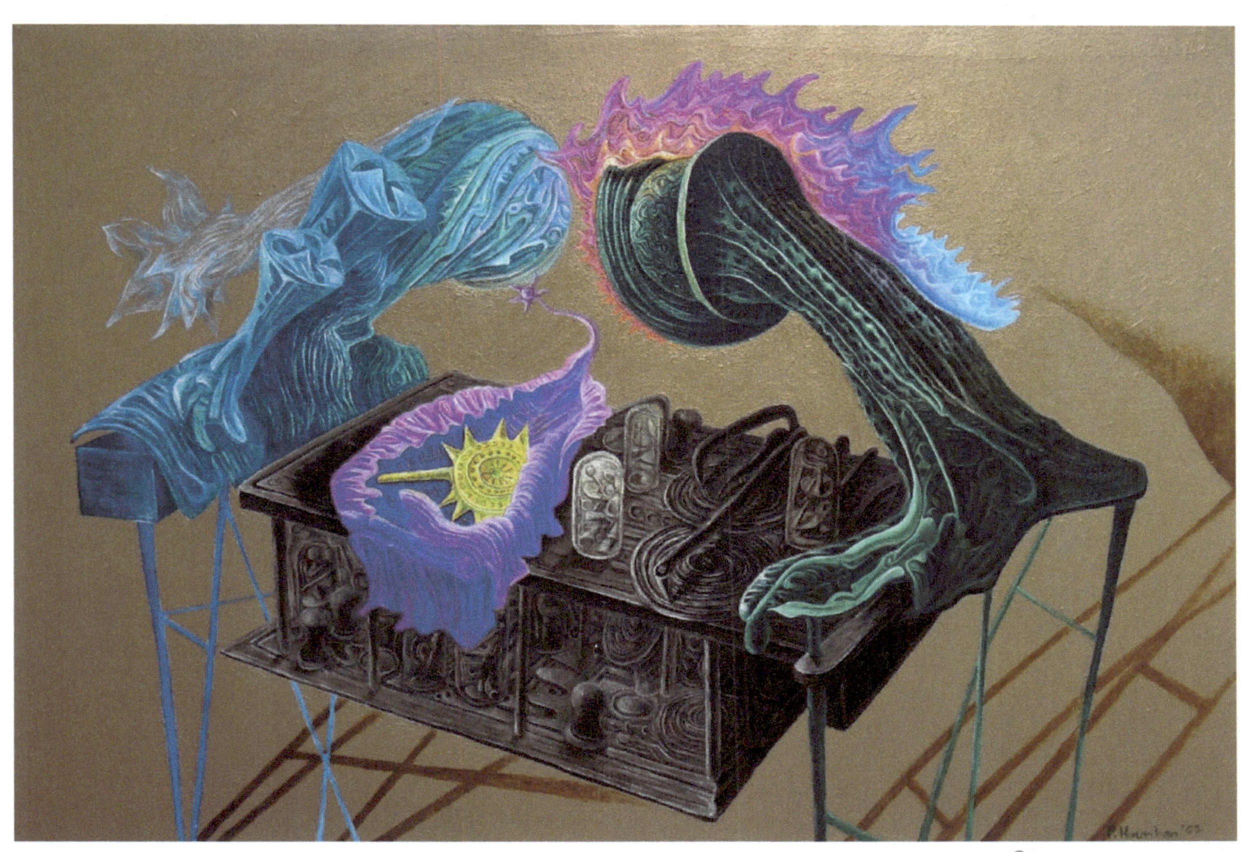

Strange parents

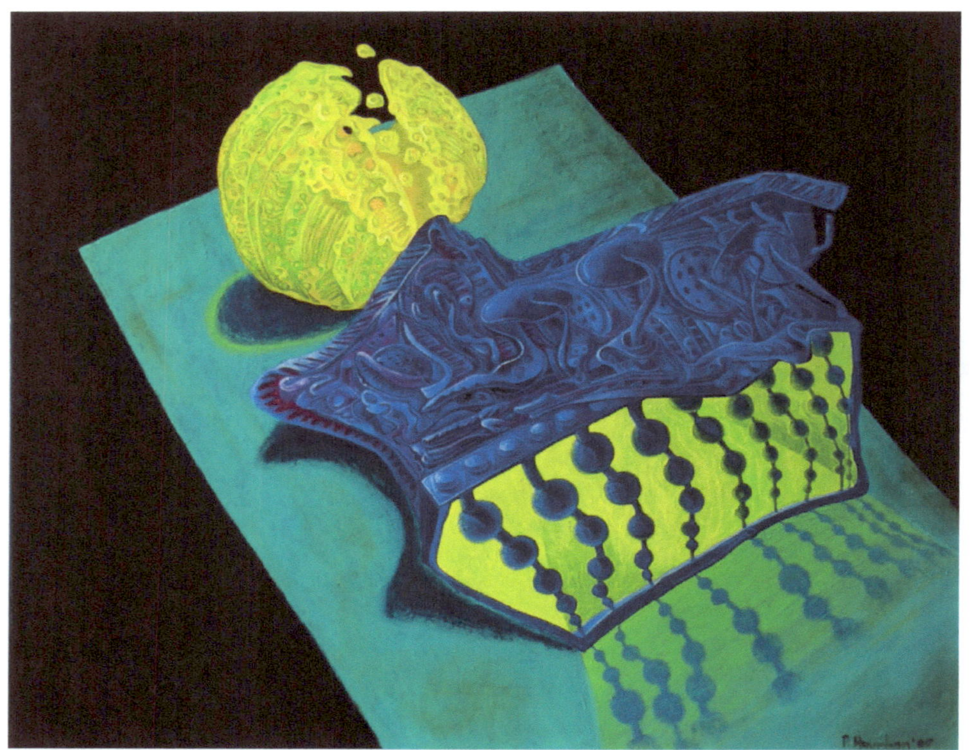

Fallen object

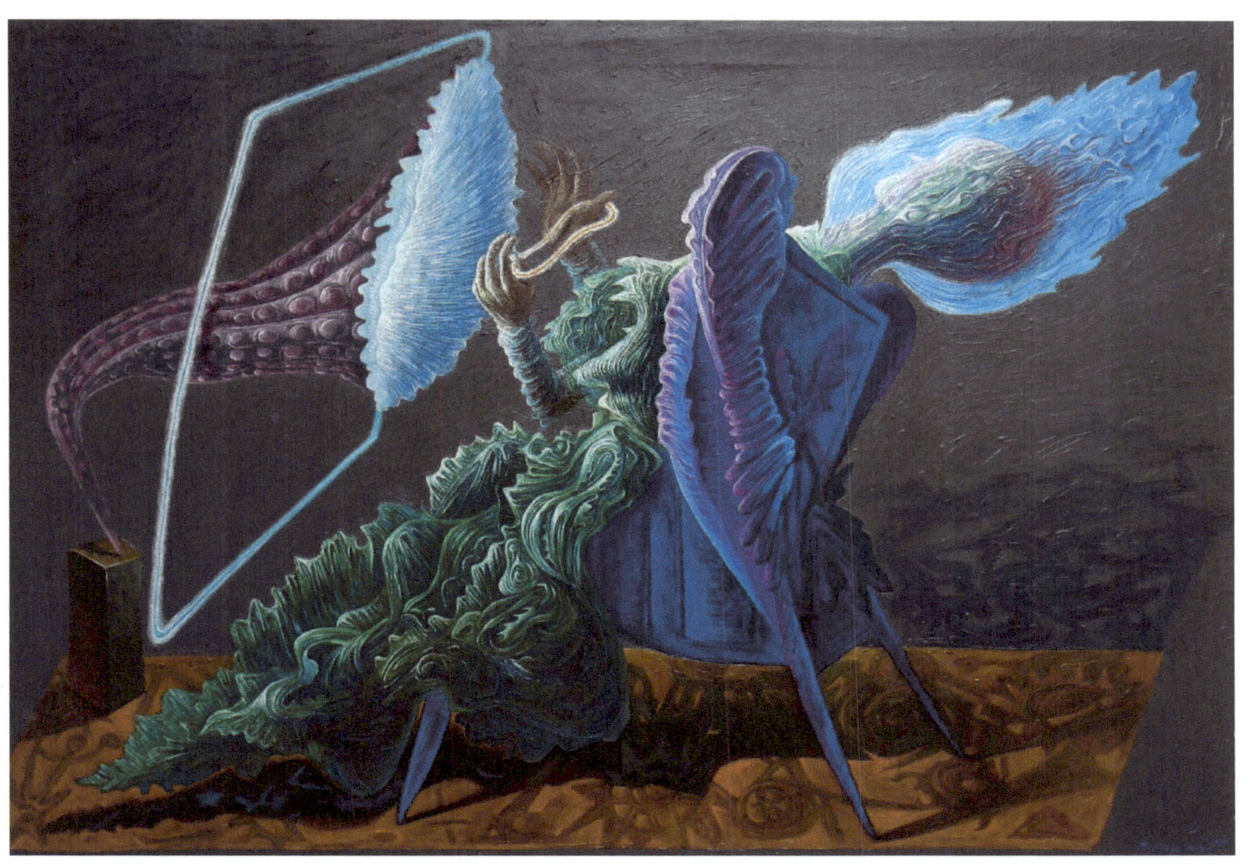

Romantic mannequin

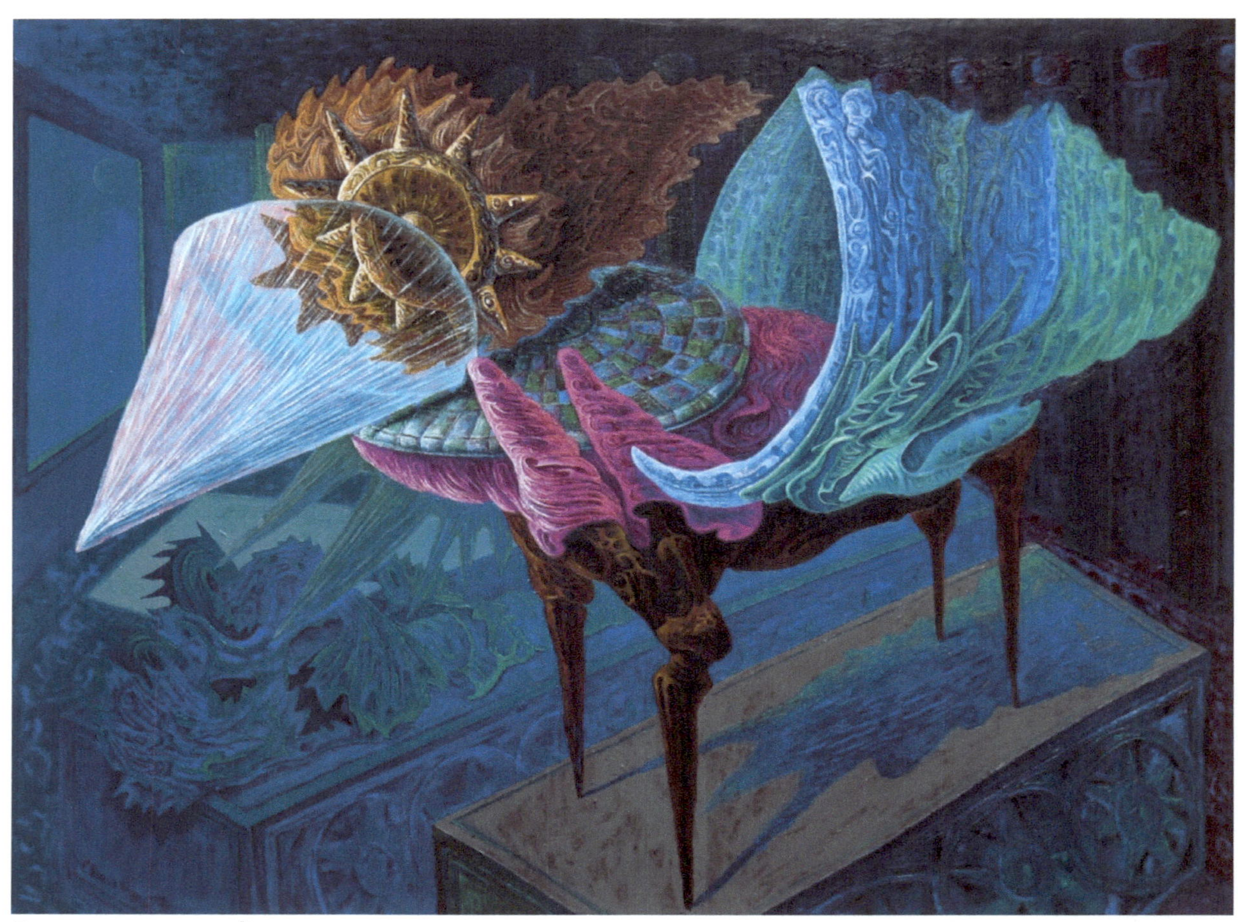

Forgotten guardian

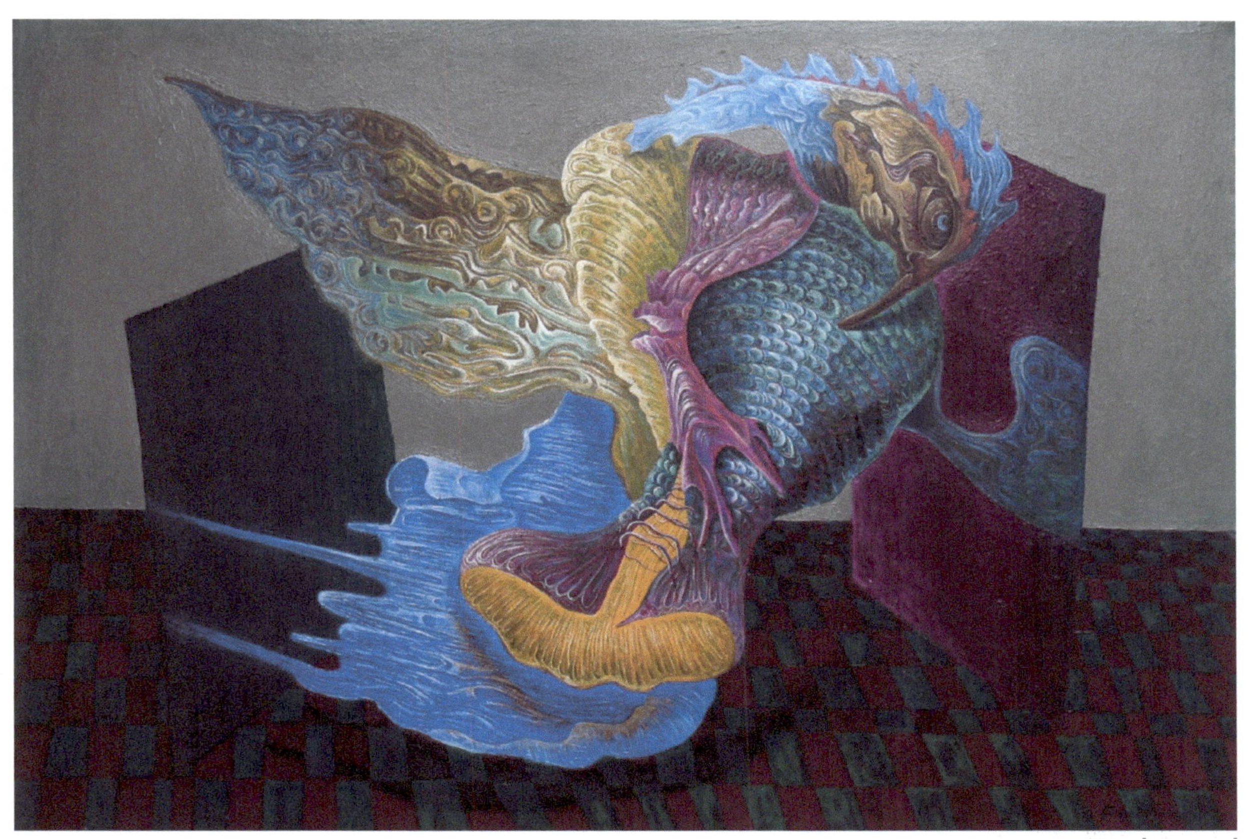

Bird angel

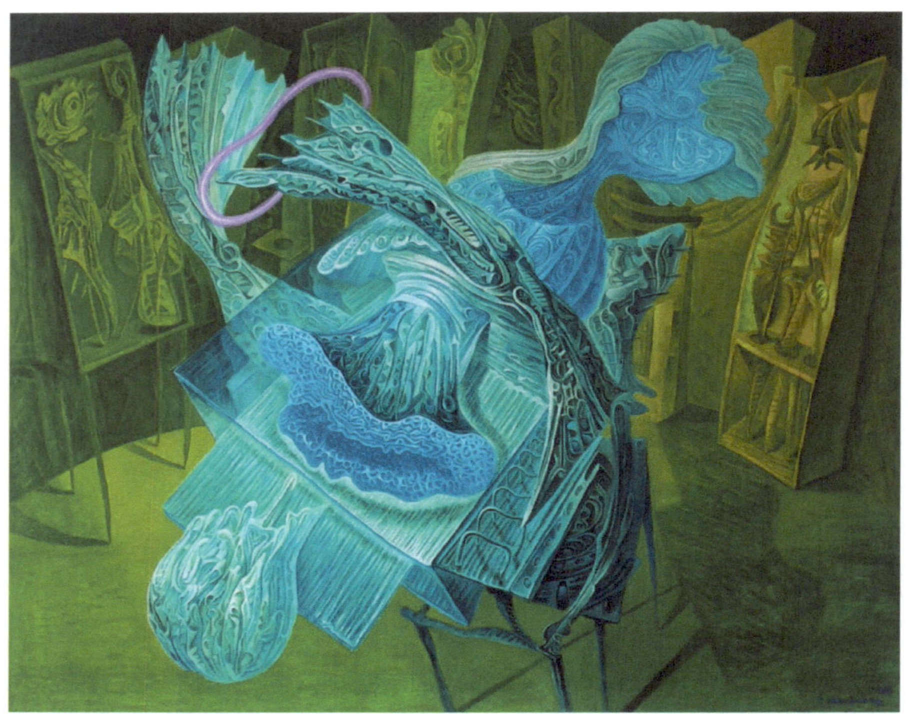
Blue machine

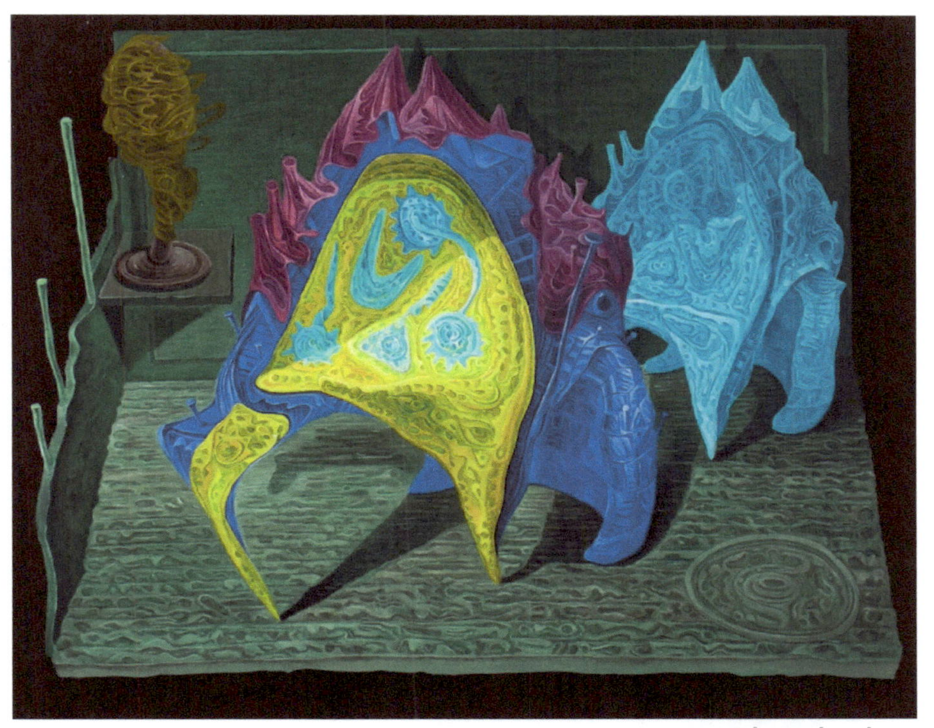

Blue shadow

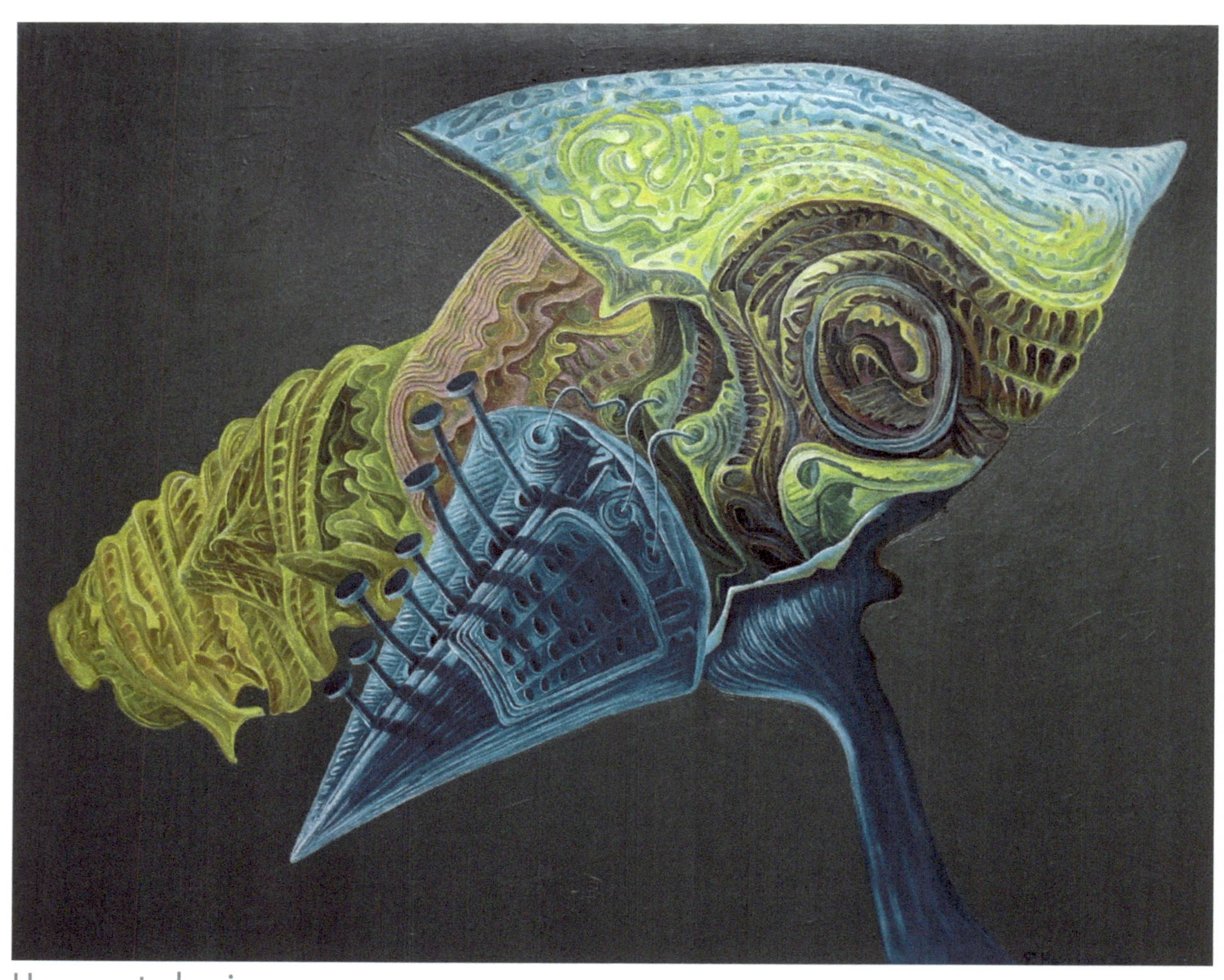
Unexpected voice

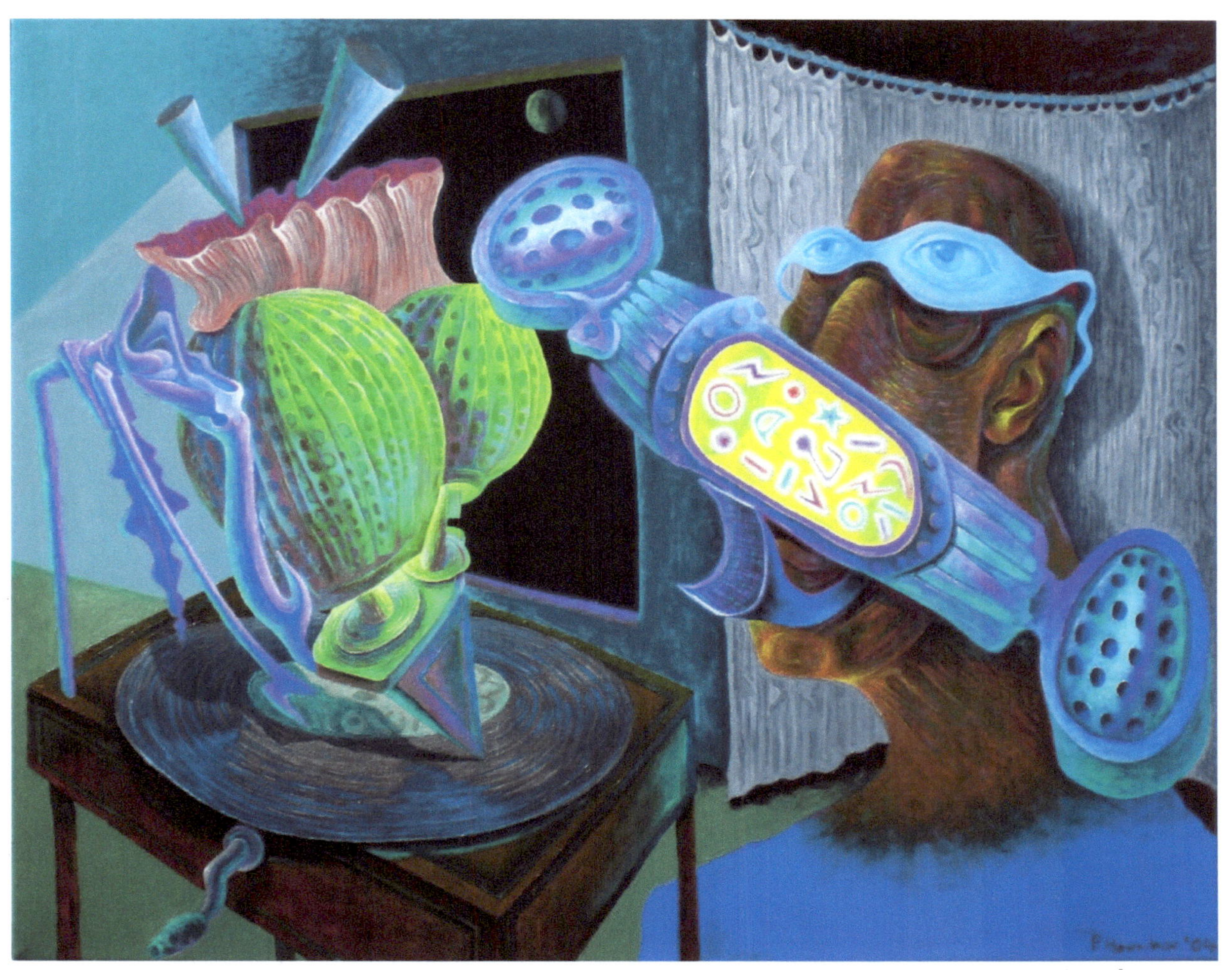

Night song

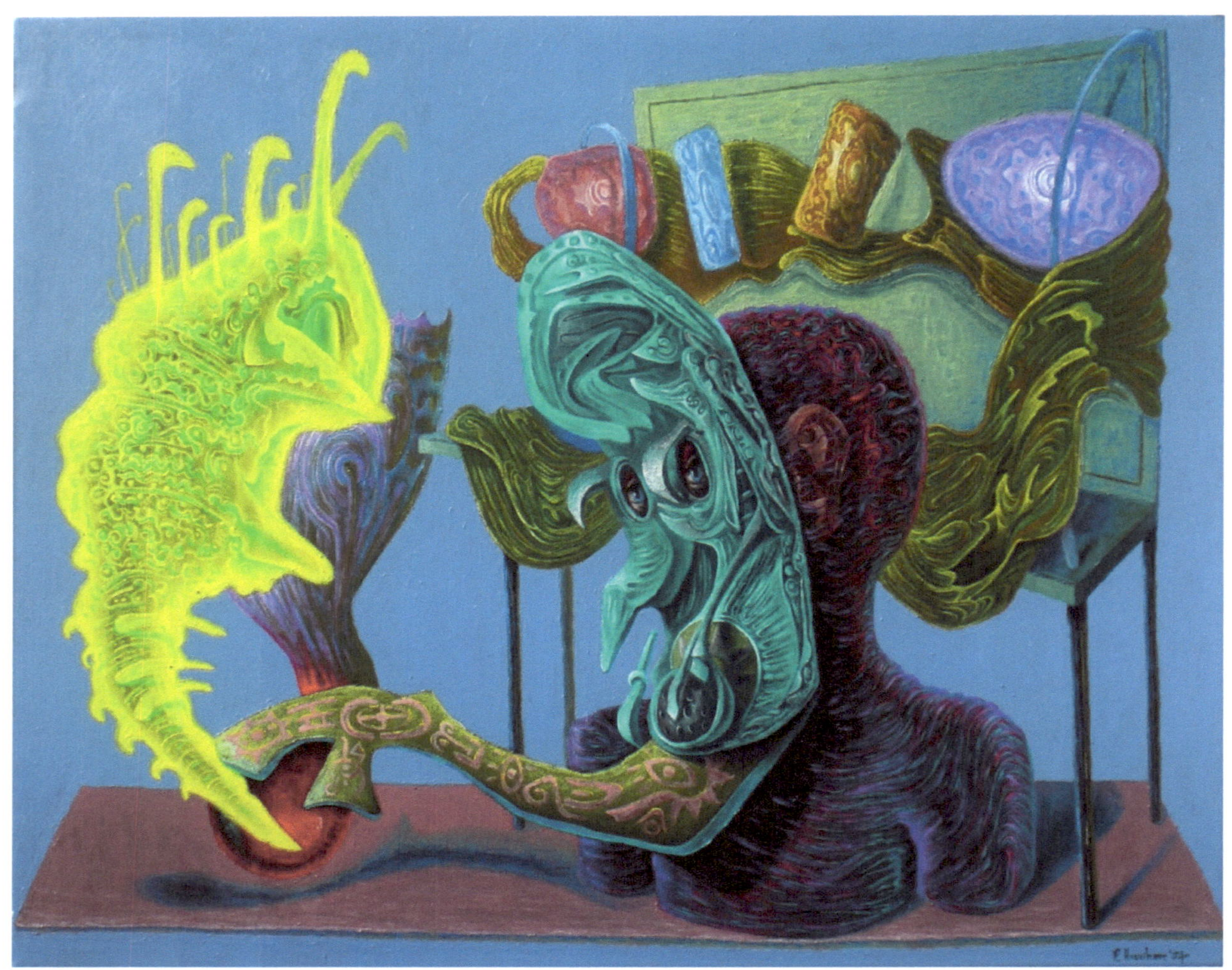

Blue mask

www.ingramcontent.com/pod-product-compliance
Lightning Source LLC
LaVergne TN
LVHW070144110826
845147LV00002B/324

* 9 7 8 1 4 7 1 7 5 2 1 8 6 *